TEACHER'S GUIDE

- How To Glorify God
- Questions on Dating
- Discipleship
- Peer Group Pressure
- Love
- What Love is Not
- Making Friends
- Honesty

for STUDENT RELATIONSHIPS

Volume 2

WRITTEN BY
DAWSON McALLISTER
AND
TIM KIMMEL

ISBN 0-86606-403-6

ROPER PRESS, INC.
Dallas, Texas

CONTENTS

HOW TO GLORIFY GOD
Lesson 1

(Discussion Manual pages 1-10)

Introduction:

To begin our discussion of glorifying God it is important that the students see glorifying Him as a life goal--above all other goals. That does not diminish the importance of other life goals, but puts them into perspective. If a student is committed to glorifying God in all areas of his life, he will be better equipped to set priorities in the various other parts of his life.

Transparency #1

Key Principles:

1. To help the students realize that God is absolute and eternally great in all that He is and does in all of creation.

2. To help the students see the importance of being thankful to God for that truth.

3. To show God and others His greatness by our attitudes and actions of praise and obedience.

Project A:

Take a piece of paper and a pencil (provided by teacher) and answer the following question: What is the main goal of your life? They may have two or three--have them list them. List all of their responses on a chalkboard or overhead projector. If the response is limited, you may want to take some ideas from the list on page 2 of the Discussion Manual.

State that as important as those goals may be, apart from a relationship with God they have little or no <u>eternal</u> meaning. We want our life to count for time and for eternity, and it can by putting God in proper perspective in our lives.

These charts may help illustrate your point.

1.
```
┌──────────────┐
│ Main Goal ?  │
└──────────────┘
        │
┌──────────────┐
│Glorifying God│
└──────────────┘
        │
┌──────────────┐
│Other Interests│
└──────────────┘
```

2.
```
┌──────────────┐
│ Main Goal... │
└──────────────┘
        │
┌──────────────┐
│Other Interests│
└──────────────┘
        │
┌──────┐
│ God  │
└──────┘
```

3.
```
        Glorifying God
┌───────┐         ┌──────────┐
│ Goals │         │  Other   │
└───────┘         │Interests │
                  └──────────┘
       ┌──────────┐
       │  Other   │
       │Interests │
       └──────────┘
```

Those three charts depict ways we can organize our lives. In the first two charts God plays a part in the person's life. He may even play a significant part. But He is not the most important part of the person's life. In the third chart, the person has placed the goal of glorifying God as a sort of umbrella over his life, under which all other areas of his life function. That person wants God to be glorified in all parts of his life, the important areas as well as the insignificant areas.

The Bible teaches that our main purpose in life is to glorify God and to enjoy Him forever. (Repeat this statement, then have the students repeat it with you.)

Transition:

In order for us to have God in the proper perspective in our life, we need to know what it means to glorify God.

I. What Does it Mean to Glorify God?

Principle 1:   (DM* page 9):

We must come to the realization that God is absolute and eternally great in all that He is and does in all of creation.

Read Psalm 19:1-6. What do these verses state is a clear evidence of God's power?

Read Romans 1:19-20. List observations that man can have of God. What are the consequences of man's observing nature and God's power?

Read John 15:12-13. What is another way we can see that God is absolute and eternally great? (By seeing His willingness to give up the life of His Son our our behalf.)

Transition:

To merely acknowledge God's absolute power and eternal greatness is not enough. For us to understand what it means to glorify God takes more than just knowledge.

Principle 2:

We need to be eternally thankful to God for those truths about Himself. God is pleased when we take the knowledge of who He is and reflect it back to Him in thanksgiving. When we are thankful, it is evidence that we have that knowledge.

*Discussion Manual.

Project B:

   <u>Thanksgiving Inventory</u>--Have students list three things about God that they are thankful for. Next have them list three things God has done for them that they are especially thankful for.

   Have one or two of them mention some of the items on their lists. Tell them how important it is to share those with God in prayer. Ask for volunteers to briefly pray and thank God for the items on the Thanksgiving Inventory. You close with your list.

Transition:

   If we know that God is absolute and eternally great and are thankful for that truth, it should cause a response from us. Therefore, knowing and being thankful for who God is should help us go a step further.

Principle 3:

   We need to show God and His greatness by our attitudes and actions of praise and obedience.

Transparency #2

   James 2:19-20 uses some strong language to explain that a deep understanding of and faith in who God is should bring about a difference in the way we live.

   Read James 2:19-20.

   1. Put this passage into your own words.

   2. What do our actions communicate about our faith?

Teacher's Note:

   It is important that the students understand that James is not saying that we have to work to earn our salvation. Our works demonstrate that we are saved. Having to work for our salvation would be in direct contradiction to Ephesians 2:8-9. The point he is making is that if we have a <u>genuine</u> belief in <u>who</u> Christ is and what He has done for us, it will be evidenced by our actions and attitudes.

   An illustration: When a person is brought into an emergency room after having been in a serious automobile accident, the doctor immediately checks his vital signs for evidence of life. He puts his stethoscope on the man's chest and listens for a heartbeat. If he hears none, he pronounces the man dead. James is saying that allowing God to change the way we think and act is evidence that He is in our lives. If there is no evidence that God is in our lives, it is because He <u>is</u> <u>not</u>. At this point you may want to mention that you would be glad to talk with any student privately if he's not sure about his salvation.)

1 Peter 4:11:

> "Whoever speaks, let him speak, as it were, the utterances of God; whoever serves, let him do so as by the strength which God supplies; so that in all things God may be glorified through Jesus Christ, to whom belongs the glory and dominion forever and ever. Amen."

This is a clear statement saying God wants to be glorified in every area of our lives. Another good verse is--

1 Corinthians 10:31 (Teacher: use your answers as personal illustrations to kids, DM page 10)

1. Think to yourself of activities in your life that may not be bringing glory to God (that may not be showing that you have a sincere respect for God and who He is).

2. Of the things that you are doing, what changes would you make to bring more glory to God?

Personal Application:

Have the students fill in these statements on a piece of paper.

I want to glorify God more when I _____.

One way I can glorify Him more in this area is by _____.

I want to ask God right now to enable me to carry out this plan to glorify Him more. (Have them silently in their hearts ask God for help.)

I want to solicit help from _____ to hold me to this program.

Encourage each student to choose a parent or friend and solicit his assistance in helping to overcome an area in which he is falling short of glorifying God in his life.

Closing Prayer:

Acknowledge that God is absolute and eternally great, a God worthy to be glorified. Thank Him for helping us know this truth about Him, and ask Him to help us communicate our love for Him through our attitudes and actions.

HOW TO GLORIFY GOD
Lesson 2
(Discussion Manual pages 11-20)

II. *Why Should We Glorify God?*

Teacher's Note:

In the last lesson we established what it means to glorify God, and emphasized that glorifying God in our attitudes and actions should be our main motivation in life. The purpose of this lesson is to establish five reasons why glorifying God is a legitimate expectation for a believer. The importance of glorifying God can not be overemphasized. It is crucial to our everyday life and happiness.

Introduction:

Remind the students that we are studying glorifying God. We will spend three weeks on this subject. It is important that we remember and retain the principles, as they are fundamental to a successful Christian walk. Review the three principles developed in the last lesson. We discussed what it <u>means</u> to glorify God:

1. First, it is a realization that God is absolute and eternally great in all that He is and does;

2. Second, it means being thankful to God for this truth about Himself;

3. Third, it means showing His greatness by our attitudes and actions of praise and obedience.

Transition:

Too often we are told to do something without a thorough explanation. In this time we spend together, we want to look at five specific reasons God is worthy of our praise.

Key Principles:

We should glorify God because:

1. He gives us so many fantastic things that it is impossible to live without Him.

2. All creation is designed to reveal His greatness.

3. We will be happier if we cooperate with Him.

4. He has shown great patience with us as sinful people.

5. All of our future hopes hang on Him.

5

Principle 1:   (DM page 11):

   We should glorify God because He gives us so many fantastic things that it is impossible to live without Him.

Transparency #3

Key Verses:

   John 1:3

   Apart from Christ nothing could or would exist. Everything that we enjoy is a result of God's greatness and grace.

   Colossians 1:17

   This verse states that nothing could stay together if it weren't for Christ's holding it together. The particles within an atom are held together by the power of God.

Project A:

   On page 12 of your manual there is a game called "What If...." Take the various items listed on the left side of the page and write each one on a piece of paper. Put them in a small box or can. Have each student draw out one and share what this life would be like without that particular gift of God. (Some, of course, are essential to our very existence. Try to imagine what it would take to overcome the absence of that gift from God.) You may want to add other gifts to the list.

   Read Psalm 100:3 (DM page 13). Have your students answer the questions on page 13 regarding this verse. They should respond that our being on the earth is a result of God's putting us here. We did nothing. Also, this verse states that God is the rightful owner of the earth and all of its inhabitants. Because He owns us, we can glorify Him by freeing Him in our lives to do what He wants with us, to us, and through us.

   Repeat the statement on page 13 to the students.

      Without God's eternal love and greatness, we wouldn't be on the
      earth or live for even a second. When we realize this, we should
      be moved to great praise and worship over His majesty and power.

Transition:

   Besides all the fantastic things God has done for us and the fact that we could not live without God, there is another good reason we should glorify Him.

Principle 2:   *(DM page 14):*

We should glorify God because all creation is designed to reveal his greatness.

Transparency #4

Key Verses:

Psalm 8:1-5
Psalm 19:1

According to those verses:

1. *List some of the things around us that point to God's glory. (List some that are not mentioned in the verses.)*

2. *What is David's attitude toward himself after observing the greatness of the moon and the stars? (He can't understand why God would be interested in or care for man. The moon and the stars are so complex and magnificent. Next to them, man seems so insignificant.)*

3. *Even though man feels small and insignificant, God has given us importance. In what way? (We are less than God in power and glory, and yet God has elevated us above the things around us and granted us glory, majesty, and authority over the things that He created.)*

Supplemental Verse:

Genesis 1:28

And God blessed them [man]; and God said to them, "Be fruitful and multiply, and fill the earth, and subdue it; and rule over the fish of the sea and over the birds of the sky, and over every living thing that moves on the earth."

This shows that God gave man a place of authority, power, and majesty. He wants all of His creations to bring glory to Him. We were created to glorify Him. And we can glorify better when we live according to the purpose for which we were created.

Project B: *(DM page 15):*

Have the students think of a time when they observed some magnificent illustration of God's creation, and then have them tell in what way it glorified God. (An example would be Niagara Falls. They could comment about the overwhelming power and force of the water and the fact that God had to be greater than all that power in order to create it. Therefore God is magnificent and more so than something as great as Niagara Falls.)

Transition:

God gives us many good gifts without which we could not exist, and He made us and all of creation to bring glory to Him. Realizing that should bring about a response in us.

Principle 3:   (DM page 16):

Since God has designed all of creation to show His greatness, we will be much happier if we cooperate with Him.

Teacher's Note:

When God gave Adam and Eve (and all mankind) the responsibility to show His glory by subduing and ruling over the earth, He coupled with the responsibility the promise of happiness. As we look around us, we can see that man in general is very unhappy. Why? (Because we have abused the earth and other people in the earth in order to pursue our selfish ambitions.) What would happen if we yielded to God's commandments? (We would be happy because we would be fulfilling God's design for our lives.) Discuss with your students that with every action there are consequences. Sometimes the consequences are good, sometimes they are bad. But God's greatness is manifested no matter what the consequences. If we obey Him, He makes us happy. If we disobey Him, He deals with our sin but is patient with us as sinners. That brings us to a fourth principle.

Principle 4:

We should glorify God because of His great patience with us as sinful people.

Transparency #5

Teacher's Note:

Read the last paragraph on page 16 in the manual, making sure that each student understands that God owes him nothing. He must see that God is loving and patient with us not <u>because</u> of who we are, but <u>in spite</u> of who we are.

Key Verse:

Romans 2:4

What do we communicate to God when we do not consider or have a thankful spirit for His kindness? (We are saying that we don't appreciate God's gift of His Son on the cross. We are communicating that we don't think it was that great of an act to die for us.)

What should be our response to God when He is kind, forbearing, and patient? (We should repent of our sin.)

Supplemental Verses:

Romans 5:7-8:

> *But God demonstrates His own love toward us, in that while we were yet sinners, Christ died for us.*

These verses tell us that we would be reluctant to give our lives for a good person. How much more difficult it must be to give one's life for enemies!

Project C:

Think of a way God has been patient with you lately. Share it with your students. Next ask them to share ways in which He has been patient with them. Encourage the students to be thankful to God for His patience by praying and thanking God specifically for ways He showed His patience in their lives. (Pray now.)

Transition:

God gives us so much; He keeps us alive; He has designed us to glorify Him; and we're happier when we cooperate with Him, but even when we don't He is patient with us. Those are all good reasons God is worthy to be glorified. There is one more reason we would like to discuss.

Principle 5   *(DM page 17):*

We should glorify God because all of our future hopes hang on Him.

Key Verses:

Psalm 39:4-7

Have the students answer the questions on page 18 in the manual.

Teacher's Note:

The only thing that we can be certain of is God's faithfulness. Putting our faith or confidence in anything else for our eternal happiness is foolish (Luke 9:25). Because we can have confidence in God's faithfulness, we don't need to worry about what lies ahead.

Personal Application:

Ask the students to answer these questions:

> 1. *What is my biggest fear in life (lack of health, good job, or happiness, or death)?*
>
> 2. *Am I willing to glorify God by trusting Him completely to do what is best for me in this area?*

Have them pray along with you silently as you lead them in this prayer.

Dear God, I am afraid of ____ (have them think of their specific fear) ____. I know that I disappoint You when I fear something that You have under complete control. Forgive me for not trusting You with this. I thank You for the confidence that my whole future is secure in You. Help me communicate my confidence in You to others, especially in this area that I have feared.

> *Thank you. In Jesus' name. Amen.*

Closing Prayer:

Acknowledge that we should glorify God because of His goodness to us, the life He gives us, the happiness that we experience when we cooperate, His patience with us when we sin, and His control over our destiny. Ask Him to help us glorify Him more in each of those areas.

HOW TO GLORIFY GOD
Lesson 3

(Discussion Manual pages 20-33)

III.   How Do We Glorify God?

Introduction:

List the five reasons we should glorify God. (See how many the students can remember before you list them.)

1. Because He gives us many fantastic things, without which we couldn't even live,

2. Because all creation is designed to glorify Him,

3. Because of the happiness He gives us when we cooperate with Him,

4. Because of His patience toward us when we are sinful,

5. Because our whole future is in His hands.

Explain to your students that we want to look at five ways that we can glorify God. This is the lesson that takes the action that the past two lessons have been leading up to.

Key Principles:

Here are five ways we can glorify God:

1. Make sure He gets the glory in our life-style.

2. Be willing to confess our sins.

3. Praise and thank Him for who He is and what He's doing.

4. Live a holy life.

5. Bear fruit as a Christian.

Illustration:
When the Oakland Raiders beat the Minnesota Vikings in Super Bowl XI, Dave Roe was one of only four players interviewed by CBS in the locker room. The commentator asked him if this was the most exciting day of his life. He said, "No, it wouldn't even rank in the top fifty." When the commentator asked him what <u>was</u> the most exciting day, Dave went on to give a clear statement of the joy he found the day he invited Christ into his life. Even though the student may not play in the NFL, he can still give glory to God in the areas where he does play and work.

Principle 1   (DM page 20):

We glorify God when we make sure that He gets the entire glory in our life-style.

Transparency #6

1. What is one of the major problems when we attempt to give God glory in various parts of our life? (Answer: We don't always have the right motive.)

2. From page 20, what are four questions I need to ask myself regarding the motives behind my actions?

Teacher's Note:

Perhaps you would be willing to relate an incident from your life in which your motive for doing a good action was self-seeking or designed to lift you up rather than God.

Key Verses:

Matthew 6:2-4 is an excellent example of a self-seeking individual. Have the students answer the questions on page 21 in the manual.

Supplemental Verses:

Luke 6:24-26--Jesus is not saying that it is wrong to be rich, to be well-fed, to laugh, or to be spoken well of. He's contrasting here the man who does what he does in order to receive those things at the expense of glorifying God. Compare these verses with Luke 6:20-23.

See also 1 Corinthians 3:10-15.

Teacher's Note:

Please stress with the students how important this discussion really is to our motive for doing things for God. God is magnificent. He deserves glory from us, and we need to be careful to give it to Him with pure hearts.

Project A:

We've talked about giving God glory in our life-style--when things are going well and when they are not. We also talked about giving God glory with the right motives. Based on this, have the students read the questions on page 22 in the Discussion Manual. Take them one at a time. Have them write on a piece of paper or in their books their response to each question. If

God is convicting them in any of those areas, have them pray silently for God's assistance as they follow through on any action necessary to remedy the problem. If there are any questions they say no to, encourage them to free God to change their minds. Have them sign and date all of the questions to which they are willing to say yes.

Transition:

To have God glorified in all areas of our life-style is a huge goal. One of the things that gets in our way is unconfessed sin. Therefore, we need to take our action a step further.

Principle 2:   *(DM page 23):*

We can glorify God when we, of our own free will, are willing to confess our sins.

Transparency #7

Teacher's Note:

It is one thing to admit to a sin when we have been confronted with it. It is quite another thing to initiate the confession to God without its being pointed out to us first. That is a lot easier to do when we understand God's holiness. When we see how much we hurt God with even our smallest of sins, we are more apt to go to Him in confession. This unit is designed to help the student better understand God's nature.

Key Verses:

Isaiah 6:3
Psalm 111:9

Teacher's Note:

Ask the students for their definition of <u>holiness</u>. (Some of the words are in the second paragraph on page 23.) Holiness is that which is absolutely pure, moral, and righteous. Our sin grieves God since it runs counter to His very nature. Therefore, to glorify God we must be quick to remove from our life things that hurt Him.

What is confession? (Answer: Recognizing that what you did was contrary to God's wishes, being genuinely worry for your actions, and asking God to forgive you for them.)

What is wrong with these definitions:

1. *Confession is recognizing that you did wrong. (Answer: It omits the important element of a repentant heart.)*

2. Confession is admitting your action once you've gotten caught. (Answer: It leaves out the important element of recognizing that you've sinned.)

What do we communicate to God when we try to justify our sinful actions or blame others for our actions? (Answer: That we don't recognize the severity of our actions toward God, that we are not truly sorry for our actions, and that we are not anxious to reconcile with God.)

Key Verses:

Genesis 3:11-12

Have the students answer the questions in their manuals on page 24.

1. How did Adam try to make excuses for his sin? (Answer: He tried to blame it on Eve, who tempted him.)

2. How did he imply that God was also guilty? (Answer: He implied that since God made the woman and gave her to Adam, He was ultimately responsible for her actions.)

Teacher's Note:

One of the characteristics of modern thinking is that man is a victim of his environment, programmed to respond in certain ways to certain circumstances. Therefore he can not be held responsible for his individual actions. Have the students discuss this comment based on your discussion of God's holiness and confession.

Project B:

Ask the student's to respond to this situation: A boy is brought up in a home in which his mother is an alcoholic and his father is in and out of prison all of the boy's life. When the boy grows up, he robs a bank and shoots a teller during his escape. During his trial his defense lawyer explains the man's background and explains that he was only acting in a manner characteristic of his upbringing. He thinks the man can't be held responsible for his actions. (It is true that our environment does affect our behavior. But our environment is no excuse for our behavior.)

OR, discuss this statement from the famous book Love Story by Eric Segal, "Love means never having to say you're sorry." Ask the students if they agree or disagree and to defend their answers. One could easily question the sincerity of a person's love if that person could do something sinful against them and not be sorry for it.

Teacher's Note:

Read the fourth paragraph on page 25 starting, "When we confess our sin . . ." as a culmination of this discussion of confession.

Transition:

Once God has been given access to every area of our lives and we are initiating confession of our sin to Him, we should follow up with a positive action that communicates to others our genuine love for Him.

Principle 3   (DM page 26):

We glorify God when we praise Him and are thankful for who He is and what He is doing.

Transparency #8

Teacher's Note:

Explain that love is not a static emotion. It can never stand still. It must take action.

Have your students read the paragraph on page 26 that starts out, "Let's suppose. . . ." After they read it, have them suggest ways in which a person communicates that he loves someone. List them on a chalkboard or overhead projector. Some suggested items on the list could be complements, gives gifts, sticks up for you, never stabs you in the back. After they have made a good list, have them pick out one of the items to do for God and have them formulate a plan that includes a time and place for doing it. For instance, they might choose to give God a gift. They could say, "I'm going to give God one hour of quality time alone with me and His Word, tomorrow from 3:30-4:30 after school." Give them a half minute to pray and ask God for help in following through with their commitment.

Key Verses:

Psalm 34:1-3

Have the students answer the questions on page 27.

Project C:

Using the list on page 28, have a time of conversational prayer, thanking God for some of the things that are especially meaningful. They can add to the list.

Principle 4:   (DM page 29):

We Glorify God when we live a holy life.

Transparency #9

Teacher's Note:

This principle is a step beyond principle 1, but has many similarities. If you are running short of time, you could abbreviate this section (certainly not because it is not important, however).

Key Verse:

Matthew 5:16

1. What are the consequences of good works, according to this verse? (Answer: God is glorified.)

2. What could we assume would be the results of bad works in the life of a Christian? (Answer: We would make God look phony. It would lower the concept of what a Christian is in the mind of the nonbeliever.)

Teacher's Note:

Have them look at the cartoon on page 31. Have the students point out the specific problems with the little man's testimony. Have them suggest what the guys looking on might be thinking. Next read the paragraph next to the cartoon. Emphasize that our sinful actions could lead non-Christians astray and blur their ability to see their need for God.

Principle 5   (DM page 32):

We glorify God when we bear fruit as Christians.

Key Verses:

Matthew 28:18-20

These verses list several ways in which we can bear fruit for God. Have the students list them. They are:

1. Go--reach out to others.

2. Make disciples.

3. Baptist them.

4. Teach them.

Personal Application:

Suggest that the students each think of a friend who does not know Christ. Have them ask God for: (1) help--in building a bridge to communicate Christ to him; and (2) an opportunity to boast about God before this person this week. Have them pray for a faithfulness in living for Christ before this person this week.

Closing Prayer:

Acknowledge God's worthiness of our praise. Close in prayer, asking God to help your students grant Him control of their life-styles, confess their sins faithfully, to be genuinely thankful to God for His goodness, to live holy and blameless lives before others, and to seek to bear fruit as Christians.

DISCIPLESHIP
Lesson 4

(Discussion Manual pages 35-43)

Introduction

You will spend the next three lessons on chapter 2, Discipleship. This lesson will cover the Introduction, the section entitled "What a True Disciple Is Not," and two principles from the section entitled "The Costs and Characteristics of Being a True Disciple."

Start off the lesson by asking the students what people say are the exciting elements of the Christian life. List them on an overhead or chalkboard. They could mention joy, peace, meaningful activities, fellowship, sins paid for, and others. After you have made a good list, ask the students to give you verses that would reinforce some of the items on the list. They may not come up with one for each item, but this will be a good exercise nonetheless. Make sure they at least use the two references on page 35. Some supplemental verses would be John 3:16; John 14:27; Romans 6:23; 2 Corinthians 5:17; and Ephesians 2:8-9.

1. *Do you think that most Christians have those exciting qualities in their lives? (An honest evaluation would be--no, they don't have those qualities.)*

2. *Why aren't most Christians enjoying those qualities in their lives? (Answer: Because those qualities accompany a commited, daily walk with the Lord.)*

3. *What is a disciple? (Answer: A person who represents another person's thought patterns, convictions, and life-style.)*

Key Principles:

A true disciple of Jesus Christ. . .

1. *Is not made by being curious or even convinced about Jesus Christ.*

2. *Has a super love for Him.*

3. *Has a real and sincere love for brothers and sisters in Christ.*

4. *Denies himself.*

5. *Deliberately chooses the way of the cross.*

6. *Spends his life following Christ.*

7. *Stays in God's word.*

Have the students answer the questions on pages 35 and 36. Tell them that before we discuss the caracteristics of a true disciple, we want to contrast a true disciple with two types of people who are not disciples.

I. What a True Disciple Is Not

Principle 1   *(DM page 37):*

Being curious or even convinced about Jesus Christ does not make you one of His disicples.

Transparency #10

Key Verses:

John 6:24-71

Teacher's Note:

This passage is too lengthy to read or discuss in depth. You should read it in advance and summarize its contents. The point of the passage that is applicable here is that these people were following after Jesus in hopes that they might receive a blessing or a miracle on their behalf, but were not interested in His true purpose in coming to earth. Jesus represented a sideshow that one enjoyed for a while and then ignored. Read what Jesus said in John 6:29. Believing should bring about a change in life-style (see James 2:17-20).

Have the students pick out the characteristics of Mr. Curious from the paragraph at the bottom of page 37. Make sure they understand that Mr. Curious is <u>not</u> a Christian. Because you may have a "Mr. Curious" in your class, communicate this principle clearly but with sensitivity.

    1. What is the difference between Mr. Curious and Mr. Convinced?
       (Answer: Mr. Convinced <u>is</u> a Christian. Mr. Curious is not a
       Christian, but may be deluded into thinking he is.)

    2. What are the characteristics of Mr. Convinced?
       (Answer: Draw them out of the paragraph on page 38--received
       Christ, has areas of his life that he refuses to surrender to
       God, won't deny Christ but will refuse Him access into certain
       areas, frustrated, is satisfied to stay unhappy and ineffective.)

Transition:

A disciple must go beyond the curious stage and the convinced stage. But before one can be a true disciple of Christ, he needs to consider the cost of such a commitment. There are six characteristics of a true disciple that we want to look at. We will look at the first three in the remainder of this lesson, and the last three will be the topic of our next lesson.

II. The Costs and Characteristics of Being a True Disciple

Principle 2   (DM page 39):

A true disciple of Jesus Christ has a super love for Him.

Key Verse:

Luke 14:26

Teacher's Note:

This verse has been greatly misused and misunderstood. Jesus is not saying that we should display malice or ill will toward parents or siblings. That would contradict other parts of the Bible. He is using the word "hate" here as a contrasting word. Our love for Christ should be so great that there is no comparison of it to the love we have for members of our family. This is a very difficult commandment to carry out since we love our family members so much. He is not saying to love them less, but to love Him more. With that in mind, have the students answer the questions in their books. Give them five minutes. Ask for volunteers to read their answers.

Project A: (DM page 40):

Have the students fill in the blanks on the "Love Inventory for Christ." Since this could be quite personal, do not ask the students to disclose their responses. Pray briefly, asking God to help us develop a greater love for Jesus Christ than we have for anything or anyone else. Use Paul's statement in Philippians 3:8a in your prayer.

Or, have the students fill in their responses to the question asked at the top of page 41 in the manual. In addition, have them think of a specific way they could show Christ that they love Him throughout this week. Have them pray, asking God for assistance in displaying this new behavior of love toward Him.

Principle 3:   (DM page 41):

A true disciple of Jesus Christ has genuine and committed love toward his brothers and sisters in Christ.

Transparency #11

20

Key Verse:

John 13:35

Supplemental Verses:

1 John 4:7-8,11

Teacher's Note:

The statements on page 42 in the manual are communicating a profound point. "Religious" activities apart from a genuine love for our brothers and sisters in Christ are useless. Have a brief discussion concerning these statements. Quiz your students on what the author is trying to communicate. Do not move on until you are certain that they understand.

Project B: (DM page 43):

Have the students read and respond to the question following 1 John 3:16. Have them select from the list below two or three practical ways to show love. Help them be specific. Have them place an individual and an action with the item. For instance, "I'm going to avoid an argument with my dad this week by doing all of my chores plus wash his car without being asked to do them." Make sure that it can be acted on this week. You may want them to use the "buddy system" to hold one another accountable. Have each arrange a time to call his "buddy" that week to see how he is following through with his commitment.

Principle 4:   (DM page 44):

A true disciple of Jesus Christ is one who denies himself.

Transparency #12

Teacher's Note:

Have the students briefly discuss the cartoon. Ask them to list things that would make up the blocks labeled "My Interests." List them on an overhead or chalkboard. Ask them for examples of "Christ's Interests."

Key Verse:

1 Peter 4:2

Project C: (DM page 45):

You may want to encourage the students to take time at home to take the "Deny Yourself Inventory." Or write each sentence on a different piece of paper and put it in a can or box. Have the student pull one out and write *down on a piece of paper his response to God. (If you have more students than statements, write some statements twice or make up other ones.) Some may have a struggle writing down anything substantial. Give then half a minute to pray, encouraging them to ask God to become the complete ruler in that area of their lives.*

Transparency #13

Teacher's Note:

Besides the misconception developed at the top of page 46 in the manual, another typical (and dangerous) misconception about dying to self is that we must annihilate any part of our personality, talents, or abilities that was dominant in our lives before we became Christians. God wants our personalities, talents, and abilities submissive to Him. He does not want to destroy them, He wants to develop them to conform to His holiness. Communicate those two misconceptions as you look at the Key Verse and answer the questions that follow it on page 46.

Key Verse:

Matthew 10:39

Personal Application:

Review the main points (God wants us to be more than curious and more than convinced. He wants us to be his disciples. He will demonstrate we are His disciples by loving Him supremely, loving His family, and denying ourselves.) Remind them of the specific projects they committed themselves to on page 43 in their manuals.

Closing Prayer:

Thank God that He wants us to be His disciples. Ask Him to show you how to increase your love for Him and His family, and to free you to give Him control of every area of your life.

DISCIPLESHIP
Lesson 5

(Discussion Manual pages 47-56)

Introduction:

Review the three characteristics of a true disciple that you discussed in lesson 4. List them on an overhead or chalkboard. Place the Key Verses beside each characteristic. Ask them how well they followed through on their projects for showing more love. Keep things light here--some of the students may not have followed through, or they may have failed. Avoid statements that would accentuate their guilt. Encourage them to continue those actions of love this week.

Introduce this week's lesson by adding the three final characteristics to the three that you already have listed (they are the three Key Principles). Remind them that God has commanded us to be His disciples, and it pleases Him when we go beyond the convinced stage to that of a true disciple.

Key Principles:

5. A true disciple deliberately chooses the way of the cross.

6. A true disciple spends his life following Christ.

7. A true disciple stays in God's Word.

Principle 5   *(DM page 47):*

A true disciple deliberately chooses the way of the cross.

Teacher's Note:

One of the hardest concepts to communicate to modern students is the concept of sacrifice. Modern youth culture teaches young people to take, not to give, and yet "giving" is the whole point of Christ's message to the world. He gave His life for us, and He asks for our lives in return. When we give Him our lives, He gives us abundant life back. We can't out-give Him. But we must _give_. We cannot be His disciples until we know what it is like to give up ourselves to choose the path of the cross. The following illustrations might help you develop a platform for the development of this principle.

Illustration:

1. You could tell them the story of the brave missionaries who went deep into the Ecuadorian jungles to attempt to bring the gospel to the head-hunting tribe of Indians called the Aucas. Relate that each man was killed on the beach of the river. Tell them how the wives of those men went back to where their husbands left off and reached that

same tribe. Today there is a flourishing church among the Auca Indians. Ask them about the sacrifice that the men made. Get their impressions on the sacrifice the men's wives made.

2. A humorous illustration is the conversation that is said to have taken place between a hen and a hog when they passed a church and observed the subject of the pastor's sermon: "How Can We Help the Poor?" After a moment's reflection the hen said, "I know what we can do. We can give them a ham and egg breakfast." The hog protested, saying, "The breakfast would be only a contribution for you, but for me it would be a total commitment!"

3. This poem from The Brethren Evangelist contrasts the life of self with the life of sacrifice.

I counted dollars while God counted crosses,
I counted gains while God counted losses,
I counted my worth by the things gained in store,
But He sized me up by the scars that I bore.

I coveted honors, and sought for degrees;
He wept as He counted the hours on my knees;
I never knew until one day by the grave
How vain are the things that we spend life to save;
I did not yet know until my loved one went above
That the richest is he who is rich in God's love.

Key Verse:

Matthew 16:24

Teacher's Note:

Have the students answer the questions to this verse. Explain to them that it is sometimes difficult for us to understand what a crucifixion is like since it is an ancient form of capital punishment. Maybe that explains why people who don't even claim Christ as their Savior can easily wear crosses around their necks. Have them think of an electric chair. Quote Matthew 16:24, inserting "electric chair" for "cross." Ask them what they would communicate to themselves and to others if they wore a gold or silver electric chairs around their necks. Although this discussion might seem peculiar, it could help your students see the violent and sacrificial nature of the cross, and would help them get a clearer grasp of what God means when He says "take up your cross daily and follow me."

Make sure the students understand the conflict waging between the Holy Spirit and our sin nature.

Transparency #14

Key Verse:

2 Corinthians 5:15

24

Supplemental Verses:

Galatians 2:20
Colossians 3:1-3

Project A: (DM page 49):

Make a list of some things, events, or people that hurt you because of how sinful they are. (Be careful that this is not a time to gossip or indiscreetly criticize individuals.) The list at the bottom of the page may help you. Ask for some volunteers to tell why those things or people hurt them. Using yourself as an example, relate how you battle in a particular area and how Satan uses guilt to make you feel worse. Remind them that Jesus already died for your sins in order to give you victory over them. Draw a cross over the list and remind them that it is Christ's victory for them on the cross that will give them the victories over the "crosses" they are called to bear.

Teacher's Note:

Have the students answer the question "How far am I willing to follow Jesus . . . ?" (DM page 50). Although God may never call on them to give their physical lives for Him, He wants us to be willing to give them nonetheless. Allow a minute of silent prayer as they offer God everything--including their lives. Close simply with "Amen."

Transition:

We need to give God every part of us. But it is important that we realize that giving is an ongoing responsibility. Christ wants us to take up His cross, and He also wants us to be prepared to carry it wherever He leads. That brings up our second principle.

Principle 6   (DM page 51):

A true disciple of Jesus Christ is one who spends his life following Christ.

Transparency #15

Key Verse:

Matthew 16:24 (emphasize "follow")

   1. If God is asking you to follow Him, does He have a course picked out? (Answer: Yes.)

   2. If God is asking you to follow Him, does He know the way? (Answer: Yes.)

3. If God is asking you to follow Him, does that mean He will have traveled your path first, thereby knowing what you are going through? (Answer: Yes.)

4. What legitimate reasons do we have for not following Christ? (Answer: We have no legitimate reasons for not following Him.)

5. What are our alternatives? (Answer: The only other path is Satan's path- *Acts 26:18.*)

Teacher's Note:

Principle 6 has three points under it (DM pages 51-53). Briefly discuss each one.

1. Following Jesus is not just an emotional, explosive event--it is a way of life. If your class does not relate well to an analogy from athletics, use one from their experience (getting a college, master's, or doctor's degree; becoming a doctor; writing an epic; etc.)

    Key Verse--2 Timothy 4:7

    Supplemental Verses--1 Corinthians 9:24-27

2. A life spent following Jesus also means imitating Jesus.

    Christ not only wants us to follow Him, but He wants us to walk like Him. Have the students respond to the two questions at the top of page 53 in their manuals.

3. Following Jesus means getting rid of excess baggage that would trip us up.

    Key Verse--Hebrews 12:1

Transparency #16

Project B: (DM page 54):

Make an "excess baggage" list. Divide a sheet of paper into two columns. On one column write "excess baggage"; on the other column write "discarded to follow the way of the cross." After a substantial list has been made on the left, read down it again, dittoing the statement "discarded to follow the way of the cross." Have each student pick out one or two pieces of excess baggage that he has been carrying around. Encourage him to discard it <u>now</u>. Give them a minute to pray, asking God to give them new strength by taking away that excess baggage. Have them sign and date their baggage item, signifying a commitment to God.

Transition:

It is impossible to take up our crosses and follow Jesus without having the final characteristic of a true disciple.

Principle 7   *(DM page 54):*

A true disciple of Jesus Christ is one who stays in God's Word.

Transparency #17

Key Verse:

John 8:31

Supplemental Verse:

Psalm 119:105

Teacher's Note:

Have students isolate the key points on pages 54-56 (we are commanded to remain in His Word; His Word endures forever; it is the only vehicle we have to learn the mind of Christ; and we can't reach others without a solid grasp of God's Word).

Personal Application:

Review the list at the bottom of page 56 in the manual, recalling the projects to show more love for God and for others, denying themselves, and getting rid of excess baggage. Encourage the students to keep those in mind as they grow closer to Jesus Christ.

Closing Prayer:

Ask God to raise true disciples from among your students. Pray that they will be willing to pay the price. Thank God that He has chosen and called us to be His disciples.

DISCIPLESHIP
Lesson 6

(Discussion Manual pages 57-60)

III. How to Become a Disciple of Jesus Christ

Introduction

The material in this lesson cannot be dealt with without an adequate review of the six characteristics of a true disciple in Lessons 4 and 5. Do page 57 in the manual first, then review the characteristics of a true disciple as preparation for the project on the next page.

Key Principles:

1. Before we commit ourselves to true discipleship, we should first count the cost.

2. Jesus wants us to know that He loves us and that we can only become true disciples in His power.

Principle 1:

Before we commit ourselves to true discipleship, we should first count the cost. Have the students answer the questions on page 57. (See also Luke 9:62.)

Project   (DM page 58):

Review the six characteristics of a disciple. Write them on an overhead or chalkboard. Ask for volunteers to clarify what each one means. If there are any misunderstandings, clear them up now (gently). Next lead them in developing the "pro and con" sheet. Have individuals suggest benefits of being a disciple, then help them articulate the liabilities that go with them. Try to develop a good, thorough list. Force them to think. The next step in this project should be done in silence. Give them three or four minutes to write their responses, then ask for volunteers to tell what they have written. Don't be caught off guard if someone does not want to be a disciple at this time. Thank them for their honesty and encourage them to reconsider their response at a later date.

Transition:

No matter which way you responded to the project, it is certain that Jesus Christ wants to be your Lord and for you to be His disciple. The final principle is crucial for you to understand before you take this step.

Principle 2   (DM page 59):

Jesus wants us to know that He loves us and that we can become true disciples only in His power.

Transparency #18

Illustration: Share with the students this progressive response that a Christian had to the Christian life.

    First: The Christian life is easy.
    Next: The Christian life is difficult.
    Finally: The Christian life is _impossible_!

Until we realize the difficulty involved, we cannot begin to understand what it means to be a true disciple. A true disciple is empowered by God the Holy Spirit.

Teacher's Note:

Jesus was able to submit to the horrible sacrifice of the cross only after He had submitted His _will_ to the Father (Luke 22:40-43). We too must submit our _wills_ to the Lord to be controlled by Him. Go over the material on page 59 in the manual.

Personal Application:

Refer them back to their decisions about becoming true disciples. Have them read their decisions again to themselves. Close by giving them an opportunity to take their decisions in prayer to God. That will serve as a reinforcement to their decisions (Matthew 10:32). When you think that everyone has finished praying, close in prayer.

Closing Prayer:

Thank God for this study on discipleship. Thank God for those who were willing to be honest with God about following Him. Pray for them by name.

LOVE
Lesson 7

(Discussion Manual pages 61-65)

Introduction:

The next seven lessons deal with the subject of love (what it is and what it is not). These lessons are followed by four lessons on dating. It is important that the students understand the material on love <u>before</u> they get to the questions on dating. For continuity, remind them that glorifying God (chapter 1) and discipleship (chapter 2) rely heavily on these discussions of love.

I. Why Is Love So Important?

Key Principles:

1. Being a great talker without having love equals nothing.

2. Being a great intellect and exercising lots of faith without having love equals nothing.

3. Being a totally dedicated Christian without love equals nothing.

Teacher's Note:

Page 61 in the manual presents one of the basic problems surrounding the concept of love--the meaning of the word <u>love</u>. You will not answer that question here, but use the materials on this page to clarify the problem.

Project A:

Explain that the Greeks understood that love was too big and diverse a feeling to be conveyed in one word. (You may want to do some study to give them background into the Greek words. It is not necessary for this project, but would complement it well.) Unfortunately we use only one word to describe many different feelings. Have students look at the list on page 61 in their Discussion Manuals. Have them add items to the list. Ask them the following questions:

1. Is the love we have for apple pie the same as the love we have for our parents?

2. What is the difference between those two types of love?

3. Do we love our parents the same way one loves a boyfriend or girlfriend?

4. What is the difference between those two types of love?

5. Do we love our country and our cabin in the woods the same way?

6. If we don't, what are the basic differences between those two types of love?

From our project we can see that there are many different feelings referred to as love. God wants us to love. It is important that we understand what His kind of love is so that we can experience it and show it.

Teacher's Note:

Read 1 Corinthians 13 from different translations (New American Standard Bible, The Living Bible, J. B. Philip's translation).

Transition:

Before we clarify what real love is, we want to look first at why love is so important.

Principle 1:   (DM page 62):

Being a great talker without having love equals nothing.

Transparency #19

Teacher's Note:

All of the Key Principles in the next two chapters come from 1 Corinthians 13. This is the first principle from this passage.

Key Verse:

1 Corinthians 13:1

1. How do you feel when you hear a noisy gong or a clanging cymbal being played all by itself? (Answer: Irritable, like something important is missing.)

2. How is that a good illustration of an eloquent person who preaches without love? (Answer: It makes you feel a lack of respect for him because you feel he is speaking for his own benefit and reward.)

3. What ingredients does love add to our conversation, sermons, and so on? (Answer: Sincerity, concern for others, respect for authority.)

Supplemental Verses:

Matthew 6:5-8 (Matthew 6:1-18 relates well to all three Key Principles.)

1. What was Jesus accusing the hypocrites of doing? (Answer: Praying eloquent prayers in order to impress people.)

2. Why do you think that disturbs God? (Answer: He is moved by proper motives, not proper words.)

3. How does this relate to 1 Corinthians 13:1? (Answer: If love is not behind our prayers, they are nothing more than empty words.)

Project B: (DM page 63):

Read each situation on this page. After each one, ask students if they have ever seen or experienced such a situation. (They may not relate easily to the first one.) Ask them what people thought about Jesus Christ when He was referred to by a person lacking love. You may want to share an experience from your life when you were speaking out for God but were not communicating love for the people with whom you were sharing.

Principle 2:   (DM page 64):

Being a great intellect and exercising faith without having love equals nothing.

Transparency #20

Key Verse:

1 Corinthians 13:2

Teacher's Note:

One of the myths of modern culture is that man has a lot of the problems surrounding him because he lacks knowledge. If only he were educated, his problems would be solved. It's true that education is both important and helpful, but to rely on it for security, according to this verse, is futile. Share that idea with your students and discuss some of the problems that have arisen because of our overreliance on and misuse of knowledge (e.g. evolutionary ideas that leave out God, nuclear warfare, dangerous levels of pollution, etc.).

Another modern myth is that faith is all you need to overcome your physical and spiritual liabilities. It is true that faith is both necessary and pleasing to God. But faith, if it is not accompanied by a loving relationship with God and a loving attitude toward others, amounts to nothing. Use the three statements at the bottom of page 64 in the manual to convey that idea to your students.

Supplemental Verses:

James 2:14-17

1. What do you think James is referring to when he talks about "works"? (Answer: Loving actions that would indicate that the faith you exercise is genuine.)

2. In the illustration in verses 15 and 16, what is lacking in the person's response to the people in need of food and clothing? (Answer: Food and clothing. He is offering words when he needs to sacrifice something of his own by giving food and clothing.)

Ecclesiastes 1:12-18

Those verses depict the absurdity of a person who seeks after wisdom for wisdom's sake. Facts, figures, and even abstract concepts are useless if we do not have God's love in our hearts.

Transition:

There are many important things in life, but nothing as important as love. Eloquence, intellect, and faith are meaningless without love. Our next principle shows us another noble action in life that is futile apart from love.

Principle 3:   (DM page 65):

Being a totally dedicated Christian without love equals nothing.

Transparency #21

Key Verse:

1 Corinthians 13:3

1. List the noble actions mentioned in this verse. (Answer: Selling all of one's belongings, giving the proceeds to the poor, and being burned at the stake.)

2. What are some other noble deeds that have a good appearance, but have no meaning without love? (Answer: Giving money to church, doing volunteer work for church, memorizing Scripture, being a missionary, etc. Have students come up with a long list.)

3. Why is it that those honorable actions have no meaning without love? (Answer: Without love there are only selfish motives for doing any of them. God does not want us to be self-seeking when we are doing what we're supposed to do.)

Supplemental Verses:

Matthew 6:1-4, 16-18

1. In verse 2, what is the motive of the hypocrites when they give their alms? (Answer: They want to receive honor from men.)

2. Why do you think that is a foolish endeavor? (Answer: (1) Most men can see through your actions to your selfish motive, and (2) if God is not honored by our actions, the praise of man has no lasting benefit.)

3. When Christians broadcast and boast of their righteousness to non-Christians, how do you think the non-Christians feel? (Answer: They may feel that Christians think that they are better than non-Christians.)

4. Are Christians better than non-Christians? (Answer: No. We were all unrighteous. Christ gave us His righteousness; it was not something unique to those of us who have become Christians.)

Personal Application:

Have the students give back to you the three Key Principles of this lesson (eloquence without love equals empty words, intelligence and faith without love equals nothing, and total dedication and sacrifice without love equals nothing.) Write them on an overhead projector or chalkboard. Ask each student to honestly pick out the principle with which he has the most struggle. Remind them that without God's love behind what we're doing, we are wasting our time. Give them a moment to confess to God their disobedience. Encourage them to ask God for forgiveness.

Closing Prayer:

Remind them that in the next few lessons we are going to look at what real love is. Encourage them to examine the motives behind their actions this week. Ask for a volunteer (or pick one student) to close in prayer.

LOVE
Lesson 8

(Discussion Manual pages 66-71)

Introduction:

This lesson is a continuation of the study on love from 1 Corinthians 13. Review quickly the three principles from the last lesson that emphasized the importance of love. (Eloquence without love equals nothing, intelligence and faith without love equals nothing, total dedication without love equals nothing.) Have a student read 1 Corinthians 13 out loud to review the context from which you will be working.

Project A:

"Can of Worms." This is an excellent way to establish the basis for this study, get everyone involved, and get to know students better. Since we are studying some of the positive characteristics of love, have the students respond to certain situations where those characteristics would be expected from us by God. Make up several "situations" (I'll give you a few to give you the idea) that could call for a positive or a negative response. Write them on slips of paper and put them in a large can. Have each student draw one or more, read it, and respond. Allow them the freedom to respond honestly. Here are some suggestions.

1. Your father promised you the use of the family car for your date Saturday night. You have asked out the girl of your dreams, and, to your surprise, she accepted. However, Saturday afternoon your father's boss asks your father to entertain a client who is in town. Your father informs you that the car is no longer available unless you would be satisfied to let him drive you and your date to the party before he picks up his client. Your response is . . .

2. Your best friend is sitting behind you in an exam. Without your knowing it, he looks over your shoulder at your answers. The teacher sees him. She walks over and tears up his test for cheating and your test for letting him. You calmly respond by saying . . .

3. You have been invited to a school party by a guy you like very much. The evening is going well when another girl attracts his attention. He proceeds to talk with her the rest of the evening and then rudely informs you that he is going to take her home and has lined up other transportation for you. Your response is . . .

Make up at least one situation per student.

II.   What is Real Love?

Key Principles:

1. Love is patient.

2. Love is kind.

3. Love rejoices with the truth.

4. Love believes and hopes all things.

5. Love bears and endures all things.

Teacher's Note:

Have the students turn to page 66 in their Discussion Manuals. Inform them that they are going to be looking at the characteristics of God's love. They will learn the kind of qualities God wants them to have in responding to situations like those in the "Can of Worms." You will look at three characteristics of God's love this lesson and the two remaining characteristics next lesson.

Principle 1   (DM page 66):

Love is patient.

Transparency #22

Teacher's Note:

Review the definition of patience with students. Make certain that they understand the scope of the definition.

Key Verses:

1 Peter 2:21-23

1. In verse 21, what does "For you have been called for this purpose. . ." mean? (Answer: As Christians we are to emulate the characteristics of Christ. Christ was willing to suffer for us--we ought to be willing to suffer for Him.)

2. According to this passage, what was Christ's response when He suffered and was insulted? (Answer: He did not attempt to get even or threaten those who were tormenting Him.)

3. Why do we not have to concern ourselves with getting even? (Answer: God is the righteous judge. Every knee shall bow before Him someday. He will judge anyone who has abused His children.

Remind the students of the sacrifice that Christ made on the cross. Read to them the first paragraph on page 67 in the manual.

Project B: (DM page 67):

"Help Heidi Hassle out of a Headache." Using the situation on this page, discuss the normal reactions we would have in this situation. Next discuss the situation with Heidi responding patiently. Discuss what effect patience could have in softening the mood of her older brother and her mother. Have them discuss the answer to this question: What would Heidi gain by getting even with her brother or losing her temper with her mother? (Answer: Nothing.) Open up the discussion to include similar situations that some of your students have experienced. Discuss their responses with them.

Principle 2   (DM page 68):

Love is kind.

Transparency #23

Teacher's Note:

Go over the definition of kindness. Have the students repeat it after you. Contrast patience and kindness, using the information in the middle paragraph of page 68. You may want to make a chart that compares the two words. Remember that patience is passive, whereas kindness is active. Patience cools a person down; kindness melts a person down.

Key Verses:

Romans 12:19-21

Have the students answer the questions on pages 68-69 in their manuals.

Teacher's Note:

Have students share incidents from their lives when kindness changed the way people responded to them. Use an experience of your own, too.

Supplemental Verse:

Ephesians 4:32

Read and discuss the story "Kindness at School." Use the following questions to lead your discussion.

1. What was most important to Steve?

2. What are some of the characteristics that Steve exhibited?

3. Why did Steve's praying on his knees bring on so much ridicule?

4. What did Steve communicate to Joe by shining his boots?

Project C: (DM page 70):

Using the instructions on the top of the page, have the students make out a list of friends. If you are running short on time, shorten the list to three close friends and three casual friends. Make sure they write one or more specific acts of kindness next to each name. Have them put down a day this coming week on which they will follow through with this action. Lead them in prayer, thanking God for His kindness to us, and asking Him to help your students communicate God's kindness to their friends.

Transition:

Love is patient and love is kind. Those are two godly responses to problems and pressures. There is one more quality of love we want to discuss in this lesson.

Principle 3:   (DM page 70):

Love rejoices with truth.

Transparency #24

Teacher's Note:

Discuss briefly the definition of love that only rejoices with truth. Next discuss one of the problems that holds back so many Christian students from demonstrating a love that finds joy only in the truth. Peer pressure is one big obstacle. We are willing to compromise our convictions in order to gain acceptance. Sometimes we feel that we will experience certain rejection if we only rejoice in truth. Ask some of the following questions in order to lead your discussion.

1. What are some examples from your experience where you believe you fell short of rejoicing in truth? (Answer: Listened to gossip, cheated on tests, etc.)

2. How do you feel when you compromise the truth?

3. How do you think God feels when you compromise the truth?

4. What should we do when we take part in anything that is contrary to God's truth? (Answer: (1) Confess our sins to God; (2) clarify the truth with the people involved in the lie; and (3) ask them to forgive you for misrepresenting the truth.)

Read the statement in the last paragraph on this page. It should clarify the basis for the discussion you've been having. Tell the students that peer pressure is as old as mankind. There are numerous stories in the Bible of people torn between the truth and a compromise. We are going to look at one example.

Key Verse:

Daniel 6:10

Teacher's Note:

Because this is no doubt a familiar story to your students, don't go into a lot of deep background. The point of this story is that Daniel did what was right and God protected him for it.

Personal Application:

Use the thought questions (on page 71 in the manual) to stimulate a final discussion on this subject. You may want to insert some extra situations. (Like: What should be our response to a dirty joke, gossip, to a boss that asks us to misrepresent the truth, etc.?) Ask the students to think back over the past week or two to conversations or actions in which they compromised the truth. Do not ask them to tell those. Give them an opportunity to pray and ask for forgiveness. Encourage them to clarify the truth with any individual that may have been misled. Maybe they lied to a friend or a parent--encourage them to tell the truth and ask for forgiveness. Maybe they cheated on an exam--encourage them to confess it to their teacher and assume the consequences. Inform them that you are available to pray with them privately and to go with them to talk to anyone they need to reconcile with.

Repeat the three qualities of love that have been covered. Remind them of their deeds of kindess list (DM page 70). Tell them that they will look at more characteristics of God's love next lesson.

Closing Prayer:

Thank God for His supreme and perfect love. Thank Him that His love is patient, kind, and rejoices only in truth. Ask Him to instill those qualities in your hearts this week.

LOVE
Lesson 9

(Discussion Manual pages 72-76)

Introduction:

Remind your students that you are in the middle of an in-depth study on love. Briefly go back and review the main points of the last two lessons. The points you should cover are: Eloquence without love equals nothing; intellect and faith without love equals nothing; total dedication without love equals nothing; and (1) love is patient, (2) love is kind, and (3) love rejoices with the truth. Remind them that our principles are derived from a study in 1 Corinthians 13. Have one of the students read that chapter aloud.

Key Principles:

> 4. Love believes and hopes all things.

> 5. Love bears and endures all things.

Teacher's Note:

Take a few moments to set the stage for the study of Principle 1. Discuss the "golden rule"--"Do unto others as you would have them do unto you." Ask these questions:

1. What does the "Golden Rule" mean, in your own words?

2. What are some ways in which you like to be treated? (Answer: respect, confidence, trust, given the benefit of the doubt, forgiveness)

3. How do you feel about yourself when someone assumes you will let them down before you let them down?

4. How do you feel about the individual that responds to you with such little confidence?

5. Does Jesus treat you that way?

Tell them that the first principle we will look at speaks directly to this dilemma.

Principle 4   (DM page 72):

Love believes and hopes all things (1 Corinthians 13:7).

Transparency #25

Teacher's Note:

Go over the definition at the top of the page. Make a list on the overhead or chalkboard of all the characteristics of a believing and hopeful love. (They are: gives the benefit of the doubt, is not suspicious, willing to trust, puts hope in the future, trusts God to do a work in a person's life, is not pessimistic.) Keep this list visible as you go on to the example of Peter.

Key Verses:

Matthew 16:23
Matthew 26:34

Read the contexts of these stories about Peter in Matthew 16:13-23 and Matthew 26:31-35, 69-75. Using the list that you just made of the characteristics of a believing and hopeful love, evaluate how Jesus responded to Peter. State each characteristic as a question (e.g., Did Jesus give Peter the benefit of the doubt? Was He suspicious? Etc.). You have to realize, of course, that Jesus knew what Peter was going to do, but you should also point out that Jesus did not argue with Peter when Peter said he would not deny Him. He gave him the benefit of the doubt, endured being let down by Peter, and then restored him to fellowship and responsibility after the resurrection.

You can use those characteristics to evaluate many people in the Bible. If you have the time, try Moses (Exodus 3-4), David (2 Samuel 11), Jonah (Jonah 1-3), or Paul (Acts 8-9).

Project   *(DM page 73):*

Read the paragraph at the top of the page. With that in mind, have your students think of one person who has given them a hard time or has been inconsistent toward God. Don't have them write that person's name, but have them answer the questions, keeping that person in mind. In addition to the questions listed, have each person again go through the list of the characteristics of a believing and hopeful love, only this time personalize the questions. (Did I give so-and-so the benefit of the doubt, was I suspicious of him, was I willing to trust, etc.) Have a time of silent prayer in which they ask God for a more believing and hopeful love. Give them an opportunity to pray out loud if they want to. Close the prayer time when you think they are through.

Transition:

If God's love can enable us to be patient, kind, rejoicing in truth, believe all things, and hope all things, then we can be certain He will enable us to go the next step in our love.

Principle 5   *(DM page 74):*

Love bears and endures all things.

Key Verse:

1 Corinthians 13:7

Supplemental Verses:

1 Samuel 19:1-26:25

Teacher's Note:

There is no way you could cover all of the story of David's being chased by Saul. But, in your preparation you could go over the story and list the highlights of the conflict, especially those incidents that point to David's bearing and enduring love for Saul. There are other characteristics of love that we already discussed that you could also point out. (Another great example of bearing and enduring love is the story of Joseph and his brothers in Genesis 37-50.) After you have highlighted the story, go over the definition of a bearing and enduring love.

Key Verse:

Hebrews 12:2

Have the students respond to the questions on page 75.

Supplemental Verses:

Romans 8:31-32

1. According to verse 31, what is our only assurance of victory? (Answer: To be in God's family.)

2. Why can we be certain that God will stand by us to give us the strength we need? (Answer: If He is willing to give up His Son for us, He'll give us anything we need.)

Illustration: Use this information to illustrate how perseverance and endurance can win out. The gravitational energy of the whole earth is estimated to amount to only a millionth of a horsepower! A toy magnet in the hands of a child can be thousands of times stronger. But what gravity lacks in brawn it makes up for in tenacity. Its reach is limitless, shaping and governing the universe across unimaginable chasms of space. Its frail attraction keeps the moon orbiting the earth, the planets revolving around the sun, and the sun along with a billion other stars rotating around the center of our galaxy like a cosmic pinwheel.

> *Two frogs fell into a can of cream*
> *Or so I've heard it told;*
> *The sides of the can were shiny and steep*
> *The cream was deep and cold.*
>
> *"O' what's the use?" croaked No. 1*
> *"Tis Fate, no helps around.*
> *Goodbye my friends, Goodbye, sad world!"*
> *And weeping still, he drowned.*
>
> *But No. 2, of sterner stuff*
> *Dog-paddled in surprise,*
> *The while he wiped his creamy face*
> *And dried his creamy eyes.*
>
> *"I'll swim awhile, at least," he said*
> *Or so I've heard he said;*
> *"It really wouldn't help the world*
> *If one more frog were dead."*
>
> *An hour or two he kicked and swam*
> *Not once he stopped to mutter,*
> *But kicked and kicked and swam and kicked*
> *Then hopped out, via butter!*
>
> *T. C. Hamlet*

Transparency #27

Key Verse:

> *2 Corinthians 4:16-18*
>
> 1. *What specific advice does Paul give us in these verses for enduring problems and problem people? (Answer: Never give up. Keep in mind that our troubles are only temporary. Don't focus on troubled circumstances.)*
>
> 2. *What will be our rewards for having an enduring love for God and others? (Answer: Our inner strength in the Lord will grow daily. God will bless us forever. We have the joys of heaven awaiting us.)*

Personal Application:

Read the paragraph at the bottom of page 76 to your students. Give them a moment to pray and ask the Holy Spirit's help in learning to love.

Closing Prayer:

Thank God for His wonderful love. Thank God that His love is patient and kind, it rejoices with truth, it believes, hopes, bears and endures all things--even us. Ask Him to instill more of His kind of love into us this week.

WHAT LOVE IS NOT
Lesson 10

(Discussion Manual pages 79-87)

Introduction:

The next four lessons will be an in-depth study of seven barriers to love listed in 1 Corinthians 13. The manual provides a lot of material for each barrier, including lots of application projects. Since they tie together, there will be built-in review and a major review of the whole chapter of 1 Corinthians 13 at the end of lesson 13.

Teacher's Note:

Use the following questions to set the stage for this study. These questions are designed to convey the statements in the boxes on page 79 in the manual.

1. What is the difference between a housemaid and a housewife? (Answer: They both perform the same duties, but with different motivations. A housemaid does her chores out of obligation and fear of not getting paid. A housewife does her chores out of love for her family.

2. What is the difference between a nurse in a maternity ward and a mother? (Answer: Once again, they both carry out similar responsibilities, but for different reasons. A nurse takes care of all of the baby's needs as the mother does. But the mother does it out of a deep love for her child.

3. In the event of a fire, which would be most likely to give up her life for the baby--the mother or the maternity ward nurse? (Answer: The mother, of course.)

4. Why? (Answer: Because she loves the baby as much or more than she loves herself.)

Next, move into a new line of questioning.

5. Can a person be married and not have any visible signs of love in his or her relationship? (Answer: Yes. A legal marriage license and a consummated marriage are all that it takes to meet the legal requirements of the law.)

6. If a guy gives a girl his class ring, dates her every weekend, calls her every night, and does not talk to any other girls, is he in love with that girl? (Answer: Not necessarily. It's true that he has given certain symbols that point to a relationship, but symbols in and of themselves are only symbols. Something must accompany the symbols in order to give them credibility.)

7. If a person can have no signs of a relationship and still be married, or can have many symbols of a relationship and not be in love, what is the missing factor that determines the genuiness of love? (Answer: It is the <u>attitude</u> one takes toward the other person.

Like the housewife and the mother, a person's loving actions are the result of a loving attitude. Unloving attitudes and actions are barriers that question the sincerity of a person's love. We are going to look in the next four lessons at seven barriers that tarnish a loving attitude and cause our loving actions to be scrutinized.

Key Principles:

1. *Love is not jealous.*

2. *Love does not brag.*

3. *Love is not arrogant.*

4. *Love does not act unbecomingly.*

5. *Love does not seek its own.*

6. *Love is not provoked.*

7. *Love does not take into account a wrong suffered.*

Principle 1   *(DM page 80):*

Love is not jealous.

Transparency #28

Teacher's Note:

Have a student read the paragraph about jealousy on page 80 in the manual. Next have each person take the Jealousy Inventory Test on page 81. Have them go down the test reading each item. Encourage them to think of specific people they have been jealous of.

Transition:

Everyone gets jealous of someone sometimes. But we want to have God remove this obstacle from our lives because it is counter to His character. If we truly have His love, He can loosen the grip of jealousy on our lives. Proceed to the reasons God is against jealousy.

Teacher's Note:

Read the first reason God is against jealousy. Begin a chart on an overhead or a chalkboard to which you can refer and fill out throughout the lesson. Read the statement at the bottom of page 81 and the top of page 82 in the manual. Have the students put into their own words what the paragraph says. Write on your chart: Jealousy assumes it deserves something that it does not and implies that God cheated us.

Key Verses:

James 1:16-17

1. According to these verses, who should get credit for good things that happen to us or to others? (Answer: God.)

2. If we are jealous of something good in another person's life, whom are we ultimately insulting? (Answer: God.)

3. What is a good remedy for overcoming jealousy? (Answer: Take a good look at all of the good things God has given to you.)

Transition:

If jealousy makes us think we have been cheated, we will constantly have problems fulfilling one of our major roles as Christians.

Move to #2 on page 82 in the manual.

Transparency #29   9

Key Verse:

Mark 9:35b

1. What characterizes a servant from a master? (Answer: The master gets the glory and prestige and has certain rights. The servant has no rights or privileges.)

2. Why should we gladly want to serve one another? (Answer: Because Jesus set the example and then commanded us to follow it. See Mark 10:45; Philippians 2:3-8; 1 Peter 2:21-23.)

Teacher's Note:

Read aloud the last paragraph on page 82. Fill in your chart. (Jealousy makes it impossible to be a servant.)

Transition:

Jealousy, like love, is both an attitude and an action. After we have entertained an attitude of jealousy for a while, we are like pressure cookers. Pretty soon something is going to explode.

Transparency #30

Teacher's Note: *(DM page 83):*

Read the third statement about jealousy to your students. Fill out your chart. This would be a great time to relate an incident from your own life in which your jealousy took action. Show your students that you fight these battles, but win them only when you let Christ's love shine from you.

Key Verses:

James 3:16-17

Teacher's Note:

Encourage your class to memorize this verse. Have the students recite it out loud with you.

Have them go back to the Jealousy Inventory List they took on page 81. Have them think of at least one person who came to mind as they read the list. Using that name, or one that God has been convicting them about through this lesson, have them pray the prayer at the top of page 84. Give them a few moments to pray that prayer, then proceed.

Transition:

Jealousy is a stifling barrier to love. The next principle discusses another stifling barrier to love.

Principle 2:

Love does not brag.

Transparency #31

Teacher's Note:

Define bragging according to the statement on page 84 in the Discussion Manual. You may want to look up some dictionary definitions here. Continue your chart by adding the word "Bragging" under the information on jealousy. Go to the next page and begin isolating the reasons bragging runs counter to God's love.

Key Verse:

John 15:5

1. What would you say should be the main goal of Christians? (Answer: The main goal of Christians is to bring glory and honor to God.)

2. Can we do anything good apart from God? (Answer: No.)

3. How does bragging short-circuit our building up of God in the eyes of people? (Answer: We lie to people about our accomplishments. We take credit for something God enabled us to do.)

Transparency #32

Transition:

If we steal credit from God, we will naturally steal glory from God. Have the students briefly discuss the cartoon on page 85. What has this student done with the "limelight?" Limelight is like an x-ray: the longer you stand in it, the more people see what you are really made of. God is the only one worthy to take credit for all of the good things that happen, because they are all gifts from Him. (Fill in this item on your chart.)

Transition:

One of the many amazing things about God is that He wants to reward us for doing the <u>right</u> things that we <u>ought</u> to do. Bragging not only steals from God, it steals from us, too.

Transparency #33

Read #3 (page 86 in the manual) to your students. Fill in your chart.

Key Verse:

Matthew 6:5

1. What was the motive of the hypocrites? (Answer: To be seen by men.)

2. What is the only reward they can expect to receive? (Answer: Whatever cheap applause they may receive from onlookers.)

Transition:

We do have something to brag about, but it is not ourselves. If we understood the magnitude of Christ's love demonstrated for us on the cross, we would not want to brag about ourselves.

Key Verse:

Galatians 6:14

1. According to this verse, is there a legitimate form of bragging? (Answer: Yes, when you are bragging about the cross of Christ.)

2. Why is that an honorable boast? (Answer: Because you boast about Jesus Christ, not yourself.)

Personal Application:

Save your chart for a review at the end of lesson 13. Have your students evaluate their attitude about bragging. Have then answer the following questions in their heart.

1. Have I been stealing glory from God by boasting?

2. How would my friends answer this question about me?

3. How would God answer this question about me?

Closing Prayer:

Close by having your students repeat after you the prayer for braggers (out loud). Everyone will probably participate. After you have dismissed them, pick out two or three fairly animated students to help you in the role-play at the beginning of the next lesson. Set up a time to meet with them before the next lesson.

WHAT LOVE IS NOT
Lesson 11

(Discussion Manual pages 87-92)

Introduction:

Prepare a role-play using some of your students, whom you have chosen in advance. Meet together to go over the different roles. The characters you should include are an arrogant person (perhaps an intellectual guy or a cheerleader), a person who acts unbecomingly (perhaps a "greaser" type student), a jealous person (perhaps an intimidated, shy character) and a bragger (perhaps an athlete). Use your imagination! Have fun preparing this. Think of a typical situation in which those four types of people would be together (perhaps homeroom class, a hamburger shop, the school parking lot). Rather than write a script, have each person determine the characteristics of his individual and then form a conversation from it. Feel free to insert a lot of humor. In fact, humor can soften the blow of some of the truths you will be putting across.

Have them arrive to your class early. Relax them and pray with them. Set the stage for the class and then let the role-play begin. It should not go any longer than ten minutes. The important thing is that each character is developed sufficiently.

When the role-play is over, take each character individually and have the class point out his or her flaws. That will serve as a review (for jealousy and bragging) and as a preview of this lesson (arrogance and acting in an unbecoming way).

Key Principles:

3. *Love is not arrogant.*

4. *Love does not act unbecomingly.*

Principle 3   *(DM page 87):*

Love is not arrogant.

Teacher's Note:

Have the students suggest definitions of arrogance. After they have given a few, compare theirs with the one on this page.

Transition:

Arrogance runs contrary to God's love. There are three reasons we want to look at that tell why arrogance is not God's way.

Teacher's Note:

Begin a new chart on an overhead or chalkboard. Write "Arrogance" at the top, then list underneath each reason why arrogance is not God's way as you come to it. You will also do "Acting Unbecomingly" on the same chart.

Direct your student's attention to the first reason given at the bottom of the page (DM #87). It will probably be necessary for you to give some background here. Your students may not even relize that Satan was once the highest ranking and most beautiful of all the angels. Read to them the two passages that tell us this story (Isaiah 14:12-21; Ezekiel 28:11-19).

Key Verse:

Ezekiel 28:17

1. What two things did Satan overemphasize in his life? (Answer: His beauty and his splendor.)

2. Are looks and wealth capable of deceiving us, according to this verse? (Answer: Yes. They caused Satan's heart to be lifted up, and they corrupted his ability to understand the truth.)

3. What are the consequences of arrogance? (Answer: Ultimately, everyone sees us for who we really are.)

4. What are some of the things that our modern society says are important for success? (Answer: Good looks, lots of money and material things, lots of knowledge, etc.)

5. What is likely to happen when we make "things" such an important ingredient to happiness? (Answer: We are bound to display various degrees of arrogance.)

Transparency #34

Transition:

Arrogance occurs when we fail to look at ourselves properly. This is caused by a second problem--we do not have a proper view of ourselves in relationship to God.

Read the paragraph at the bottom of page 89 and fill out your chart.

Key Verses:

Job 38:1-7,12-15 (<u>The Living Bible</u>)

1. What do you think God was trying to communicate to Job? (Answer: That Job is not, and never will be, God. Therefore, stop challenging God with arrogant statements.)

2. If God does all of the great things listed in this passage (He does those and myriads more), how should you feel about your life? (Answer: That you are secure in Him; therefore, you don't need something as insecure as arrogance in your life.)

Transition:

Jesus had a <u>right</u> to be arrogant--He is God! But He modeled a humble example and wants us to model the same.

Key Verses:

Philippians 2:5-8

Teacher's Note:

Encourage your students to seek to be like Christ by having a humble spirit. First they should ask God to forgive them for their arrogant behavior. Lead them in the prayer at the middle of page 90 in the manual. Point out that this would be a good prayer to carry in their purses or wallets to use when necessary.

Transition:

Love is to be a positive statement of who God is and what He is like. The next principle we will look at mars God's beauty in a bold way.

Principle 4 (DM page 90):

Love does not act unbecomingly.

Teacher's Note:

Go over the definition at the bottom of the page. Write this new category on your chart.

Project:

Supply each student with a piece of paper. Have them number from 1 to 12 down the left side of the paper. They will answer four questions about each statement.

Have I Done This?	When Did I Do This?	Whom Did I Offend?	Have I Sought Forgiveness Yet?

1.

2.

Tell them to save this paper because you will be coming back to it.

Teacher's Note:

Read the statement at the top of page 92 in the manual and list the two characteristics of acting unbecomingly on your chart.

Key Verses:

2 Thessalonians 3:7-8

Where do you think we would be today if Paul had acted in a spoiled and rude way as a guest in various churches? (Answer: It is certain that we would not have a major part of the New Testament, because he would not have been qualified to instruct us.)

Ephesians 4:1-4

Teacher's Note:

The bottom line is that we are not to give the world any grounds upon which to accuse us. Unbecoming behavior destroys the unity that God wants so much for us to have.

Personal Application:

Have your students bring back the answers to the Rude Inventory Test. Instruct them to pick out an individual that they offended. Ask them to put down next to that person's name a day and time when they would be able to apologize this week. (They can write a letter if necessary.)

Closing Prayer: (DM 92):

Lead them in the prayer at the bottom of the page. Encourage them to seek forgiveness from as many people as possible on their list.

WHAT LOVE IS NOT
Lesson 12

(Discussion Manual pages 93-98)

Introduction:

Review briefly the four Key Principles of lessons 10 and 11. Ask the students how they are doing in applying the principles to specific situations in their lives. Get them to relate some of their victories. Read 1 Corinthians 13 to refresh their memories of the context.

Key Principles:

5. Love does not seek its own.

6. Love is not provoked.

Principle 5   *(DM page 93):*

Love does not seek its own.

Transparency #35

Teacher's Note:

Begin a new chart for this lesson on an overhead or chalkboard. Remember, this will be used for your review in lesson 13, so be thorough and neat. Start off this discussion by using the following questions.

1. What are some things people do to build themselves up?

2. What is the most self-seeking incident that you observed recently?

3. What did you think about the person?

4. What do you think the person felt about you?

5. What do you think the expression "seeking one's own" means?

Compare their definitions to the one given on this page. Log the definition on your chart. Have the students write in their manuals or on a piece of paper the characteristics and consequences of a self-seeking person that they glean from the paragraphs here. (Have different students read from their lists. Make sure they have listed everything.)

Key Verses:

Genesis 13:1-18

1. What did Abraham give up? (Answer: The best land, pasture, and water.)

2. Why did Abraham give it up? (Answer: (1) Because he loved Lot, and (2) because he was willing to give up something for the sake of peace.)

3. What do you think Lot's main concern was? (Answer: That he get the best land for himself.)

4. What were the results of Lot's self-seeking endeavors? (Answer: He was corrupted, along with his family.)

Supplemental Verses:

Acts 5:1-11

1. Why did Ananias and Sapphira lie? (Answer: They were greedy but wanted to put forth the appearance that they were generous and sacrificial.)

2. Is God patient with you when you are self-seeking? (Answer: Very much so. Death would not be an unfair response from God, but He is merciful in spite of our behavior.)

Project   (DM page 95):

Have the students take the Selfish Test. You may want to think up other situations to add to the list. Have them choose their most recent selfish acts. Share an incident from your own experience, then encourage them to share theirs. Pair them up and have them pray for one another. Encourage them to reconcile the specific incident each mentioned with anyone that might have been offended. Lead them in the prayer at the bottom of the page as you close this section.

Transition:

Most of the barriers to genuine love in our lives are a result of our negligence and sin. Sometimes, however, the mistakes or sins of others lead us to react in an unloving way. Our next principle deals with that problem.

Principle 6   (DM page 96):

Love is not provoked.

Transparency #36

Have the students relate the most recent time they can remember being angry. Ask them these questions:

1. Why did this get the best of you whereas other important problems don't?

2. What were the results of your blow-up?

Go over the paragraph explaining what being provoked means. Continue to fill out your chart that is outlining these principles.

Transition:

It is hard to convince a person that we truly love him when our temper has got the best of us. There are two good reasons for that:

1. Because we fail to look for the best in the other person.

2. Because our actions show that there is no answer to the problem or circumstance we are facing.

Key Verses:

Luke 9:51-55

Have the students answer the questions on page 97 in their manuals.

Supplemental Verses:

Exodus 32:15-20
Numbers 20:1-12

Use the same line of questioning to look at Moses' temper problems.

Teacher's Note   (DM page 98):

Read the statement at the top of the page. Go back to the examples that your students brought up at the beginning of this discussion. Have them suggest the solution to each that could have been available had they asked God for it.

Key Verses:

Psalm 73:21-23

1. What adjectives describe your feelings when someone gets the best of you? (Answer: Bitter, irrational, hostile, etc.)

2. What does the psalmist say about this condition of the heart? (Answer: It is senseless and ignorant.)

Teacher's Note:

The important thing to remember is that no matter how big our problem is, God is always bigger than our problem. He has everything under control.

Key Verses:

Psalm 73:25-26

Personal Application:

Read 1 Peter 2:21-25. Remind the students that Jesus had lots of opportunities and legitimate excuses for being provoked. But He set an impeccable example. We are to "walk in His steps." Close by having them ask God for forgiveness regarding their recent blow-ups.

Closing Prayer: (DM page 98):

Pray the prayer at the bottom of the page on their behalf.

WHAT LOVE IS NOT
Lesson 13

(Discussion Manual pages 99-102)

Introduction:

This lesson is the seventh and final lesson in a study of love from 1 Corinthians 13. You will only discuss one Key Principle so that you will have time to review and tie everything together at the end. The first part of this lesson should be the discussion/discovery method of teaching that we have used all the way to this point. You will probably have to use straight lecture to cover the review adequately.

Grudges have caused more problems than we will ever know. A grudge is like a malignancy eating away at the core of one's soul. As a Christian, it is impossible to grow spiritually when we have an unforgiving spirit. It runs contrary to God's love, and is therefore intolerable to Him. Besides destroying marriages, families, businesses, and good friends, grudges have a way of destroying our health, too.

Key Principle: *(DM page 99)*:

7. Love does not take into account a wrong suffered.

Transparency #37

Teacher's Note:

Point out the definition of a grudge at the top of the page. Write that on the chart you have been compiling over the last three lessons for your review.

Project:

Grudge Self-Analysis Test. Have the students take the test privately. If any student has a grudge that is not directed at anyone related to your group, encourage him to relate it. Take them through the four questions. The first step in eliminating their grudges has already been taken--admitting that they have a grudge. Next, give them a moment to take a second step--asking God to forgive them. Have them use the prayer on page 102 in the manual. The third step, reconciliation, will be dealt with later.

Transition:

God cannot stand our grudges. They inhibit His work in our lives and in others. We are going to look at specific ways that grudges wreck what God is doing in our lives.

Teacher's Note   *(DM page 100):*

Go over the concepts on this page. (God assumes the responsibility to even any score.)

Key Verses:

Romans 12:19-21

Have students answer all of the questions about those verses.

Transition:

God has not given us the responsibility of getting even. We could never be trusted with such a responsibility. He promises that if we have been mistreated, He will deal with our offenders. But He has given us a specific action to take toward our offenders, and we see it in the next Key Verses.

Key Verses:

Ephesians 4:31-32

Teacher's Note:

Once again, have the students answer the questions to the verses. God had every right to get even with us. But out of His compassion, He chose to get even with a substitute--His precious Son. Because Christ was willing to bear our guilt and punishment, we now have the wonderful gift of eternal life.

Key Verses:

Colossians 3:12-13

Personal Application:

As a final application for this lesson, direct your students back to the Grudge Self-Analysis Test. Because they have been holding a grudge toward an individual, they have most likely been responding to that person in a cold, unloving way. Encourage them to go to that person this week (or write them a letter), asking the person to forgive them for dealing with them in an unloving way. Remind them that they are seeking forgiveness--not reopening a wound. They should not discuss the other person's behavior, but rather ask forgiveness for their own. It is God's responsibility to convict the other person. It is quite likely that your students' actions will initiate God's work in the heart of the one who offended them.

Go back and capsulize on an overhead or posters the outlines of chapters 3 and 4 in the Discussion Manual. Use the charts you made the last four lessons to review the seven barriers to love.

Closing Prayer:

Use the conclustion on this page, reminding them again of the necessity to have lives controlled by the Holy Spirit. Pray for the Spirit's love to empower you to love.

QUESTIONS ON DATING
Lesson 14

(Discussion Manual pages 105-10)

Introduction:

This lesson covers the first three questions of this chapter:

1. How can I control my sexual passions when I'm alone?

2. Does premarital sex ruin a girl for Christian service?

3. How does a girl get a guy interested in her?

Although the third question might be very important to the girls in your group, the first and second questions deal with problems that more seriously endanger the student's walk with God and his/her overall happiness. If you are limited for time, therefore, priority should go to the first two questions.

I. How Can I Control My Sexual Passions When I Am Alone?

Key Principles:

1. Quit reading material that messes up your thought life.

2. Meditate on God's Word.

3. Spend more time with people who promote purity.

4. Find a Christian friend who can encourage you and pray for you.

5. Turn your sexual drives into creativity for God.

6. See your problem for what it really is--selfishness.

Teacher's Note:

This question addresses an extremely sensitive topic--masturbation. Very few adults or churches are willing to deal with the problem. Yet this is a serious problem among young people, and it causes them much guilt. Honesty is the best approach to this topic. Be cautious and discreet, but also be candid. If your class is coeducational, you will probably be wise to divide up by sexes, with a godly woman discussing it with the girls. Because the problem is more severe among boys, the man who deals with them should be extremely sensitive.

Start by asking a few questions:

1. Why do young people have such strong sexual drives? (Answer: Partly physiological--sexual hormones have come alive suddenly and are extremely active; partly psychological--when you come out of childhood, you are more

aware of the opposite sex and are developing more interest in why they are unique; partly environmental--girls' and guys' fashions, advertising, music, movies, TV, and more open discussions about sex among peers all accentuate and stir your sexual drives.)

2. Do you have to be in the company of a person of the opposite sex to have your passions build up? (Answer: No. Thoughts about a member of the opposite sex or visual stimuli can lead you to impure thoughts easily.)

3. Are passions sinful? (Answer: Absolutely not! They are normal, built-in drives given to people by God--but like all of God's gifts, are designed to be used properly. If one abuses any gift that God gives him, he can be a victim of unnecessary consequences.)

Transition:

When we allow ourselves to dwell on members of the opposite sex without a priority of pleasing God, it will inevitably lead to impure thoughts. Impure thoughts will demand gratification. At that point young people are most likely to succumb to the temptation to masturbate. Masturbation is the manual stimulation of the genitals in order to achieve orgasm. We want to discuss six principles that will help you avoid being trapped in tempting situations.

Teacher's Note:

At this point some of your students may want to debate whether masturbation is sin or not. If it is necessary to pursue debate, keep in mind that masturbation is almost always accompanied by sensual and lustful thoughts. In the case of your students, those thoughts are most likely about a person to whom they are not married. Imagining them as marital partners is an unacceptable compromise. Only until they are married can it be guaranteed that the person they are dwelling on would be their sexual partner. A scriptural argument against lust should be developed. (Matthew 5:27-28--you will be discussing this in lesson 17.)

Principle 1   (DM page 106):

Quit reading material that messes up your thought life.

Transparency #39

Teacher's Note:

Masturbation often follows or accompanies prolonged exposure to sexually explicit materials.

Key Verse:

Philippians 4:8

Finally, brethren, whatever is true, whatever is honorable, whatever is right, whatever is pure, whatever is lovely, whatever is of good repute, if there is any excellence and if anything worthy of praise, let your mind dwell on these things.

1. With what does God want us filling our thought life? (Answer: Things that build up, not tear down.)

2. How do pornographic material, sexually explicit books, movies, or music pollute a person's thought life? (Answer: By portraying a beautiful gift of God in a cheap and sensuous way.)

Supplemental Verses:

Colossians 3:1-3

Transition:

Just taking sexual reading materials or stimuli out of our lives is not enough. We have to replace them with material that builds us into what God wants us to be.

Illustration: If a person is on a junk food diet for a prolonged period of time, he can do serious damage to his physical health. Withdrawing from junk food must be accompanied by the establishment of a proper diet.

Principle 2   (DM page 106):

Meditate on God's Word.

Transparency #40

Key Verse:

Psalm 119:11

1. Why did David put God's Word in his heart? (Answer: So that he would not sin against Him.)

2. Do you think David was meditating on God's Word when he stared at Bathsheba taking a bath? (Answer: Obviously not!)

Transition:

We do not always have the willpower to resist temptation. God does not want us to try to fight this battle alone. He has given us His Holy Spirit, and He has given us a lot of supporters. That brings us to a third principle.

Principle 3   *(DM page 107):*

Spend more time with people who promote purity.

Teacher's Note:

There is safety in numbers. Sometimes the only way we can avoid masturbation is by getting with some other Christians who are committed to honoring God.

Supplemental Verse:

Matthew 18:20

> For where two or three have gathered together in My name,
> there I am in their midst.

1. What does this verse guarantee? (Answer: He will be among a group of Christians as a source of leadership, courage, and strength.)

2. What if a Christian young person does not have close Christian friends? (Answer: He needs to develop some.)

3. Who are some close Christian friends that you can spend time with? (Answer: Encourage them to think of their closest Christian friends. Remind them that a telephone call to a committed Christian friend can center their thoughts back on Christ.)

Principle 4   *(DM page 107):*

Find a close Christian friend who can encourage you and pray for you.

Teacher's Note:

This principle is vital. You may want to suggest specific people who would be trustworthy confidants. If you are willing, volunteer yourself. It is crucial that the students see that Satan wants to destroy them with guilt. Spend some time looking at the Key VErse as it applies to this discussion.

Key Verse:

James 5:16

Principle 5   *(DM page 108):*

Turn your sexual drives into creativity for God.

Transparency #41

Teacher's Note:

The emphasis of this principle should be put on creativity. A young person is tempted to masturbate because of what he has been concentrating on. If he puts that effort toward concentrating on God through creative endeavors like those listed on this page, he would relieve a lot of the tension.

Supplemental Verse:

Hebrews 11:6

This verse says, "He is a rewarder of those who seek Him." What does that mean in light of principle 5? (Answer: God will honor the endeavors of a Christian who wants to distract himself from temptation by seeking God.)

Principle 6   (DM page 108):

See your problem for what it really is--selfishness.

Teacher's Note:

Masturbation is personal gratification. But God has designed sex to be a way that we meet and fulfill someone else's needs. "Solo sex" does not fit into God's design for us.

II. Does Premarital Sex Ruin a Girl for Christian Service?

Teacher's Note:

This question should apply to _both_ girls and guys. A misuse of sex by either gender is detrimental to their Christian walk and testimony. Be very sensitive here. There may well be a guy or girl among your students who has had intercourse. They are already feeling very guilty; therefore, point out God's forgiveness as developed on page 109 in the manual.

Key Principles:

1. God wants to forgive us of our sexual sins.

2. God wants to restore us to fellowship and service.

3. We must confess our sins to God.

4. We must commit ourselves to avoiding sexual sin.

Ephesians 4:32

And be kind to one another, tender-hearted, forgiving each other, just as God in Christ also has forgiven you.

Teacher's Note:

It is not uncommon among young people to reject and alienate a brother or sister who falls into sexual sin. The gossip spreads throughout the group, and soon the individuals are ridiculed openly or given the "silent treatment." It is important to emphasize that if a person is repentant of his sin, his Christian friends should enfold him with their love (as God does) and support him in such a way that he has strength to resist sexual sin in the future. Christians are guilty if they "brand" a brother or sister unclean who is truly sorry for his sins. In forcing him out of the fellowship, they may be forcing him back into the environment that caused him the problem in the first place.

III. How Does a Girl Get a Guy Interested in Her?

Key Principles:

1. Pray.

2. Be a friend first.

Teacher's Note:

Discuss the <u>motive</u> for wanting a boyfriend. God would not be pleased if you wanted a particular guy in order to impress people, make some people jealous, have a steady date, and so on. Those are all selfish reasons for wanting a guy.

The guy should be the type that would bring the girl closer to God. His spiritual walk should be evaluated.

Supplemental Verse:

1 Peter 3:3

1. What two parts of a woman is Peter contrasting? (Answer: The outside, which can look good but be only surface beauty, with the inside, which reveals the woman's genuine commitments.)

2. Does this mean that our appearance is not important? (Answer: Certainly not. We should just be careful not to think that a pretty face and figure and attractive clothes will bring happiness to us or to a committed Christian guy.)

3. What are some ways that a girl can develop her inner spirit? (Answer: Pursue a discussion on the numerous possibilities that she has.)

Personal Application:

God wants us to honor Him in all parts of our life. As teenagers, our sexuality is especially vulnerable. Commit it daily to God. Let Him be the object of your holy passions. He will bless you for your faithfulness to Him.

Closing Prayer.

QUESTIONS ON DATING
Lesson 15

(Discussion Manual pages 111-15)

Introduction:

All four of the questions in this lesson are critical to teenagers. However, you should try to evaluate the greatest needs of your students and concentrate in those areas. Question 6 on how far can a couple go sexually is a lesson in itself. Spend adequate time on this question. Question 7 is important in that it could help girls understand how they often tease guys by the way they act or dress. Some of your students might be thinking of marriage soon. Make them evaluate the issues on question V.

IV. Why Do Guys Slowly Drop Girls, Instead of Coming Right Out and Telling Them It's Over?

Transparency #42

Teacher's Note   *(DM page 111)*:

Sometimes a guy wants to end a romance but keep a friendship intact. A gradual change in his romantic actions is designed to communicate a change in interest but not in friendship. For some girls, that method might actually cause the least pain. But it is true that in the majority of cases, an honest discussion of feelings is best.

Project A:

Have two guys or two girls debate this issue. They should address the following questions:

1. Which way would you like to be let down, quickly or slowly?

2. Why?

3. Which way is the most difficult for you?

4. Why?

5. What would be a good way to avoid hurting feelings unnecessarily? (Answer: Put the emphasis of your relationship on Jesus Christ, not romance.)

Teacher's Note:

Have the students discuss the questions below as a group or in small groups. Formulate some principles from their discussion. Write those on an overhead or chalkboard.

1. What are some things girls could do to keep a guy from feeling trapped?

2. What can guys do to keep from getting trapped?

3. What considerations should a guy have when breaking up with a girl?

4. How can a couple maintain a friendship after they have broken up?

V. Why Do Some People Rush into Marriage?

Transparency #43

Key Principles:

1. Some feel that marriage is another step up the ladder of social success.

2. Some people feel that marriage will solve their problems.

3. Many responsibilities are often overlooked.

Teacher's Note:

Have students write down on a piece of paper what they consider the ideal ages for a guy and girl to get married. Collect their answers and share them with the class. Compute the class average. Next have a brief discussion as to why they selected the ages they did.

Principle 1 (DM page 112):

Some feel that marriage is another step up the ladder of social success.

1. Is marriage designed as a vehicle for social success? (Answer: Not primarily. Marriage is a vehicle through which a man and a woman can achieve the maximum expressions of love in an environment that balances freedom with responsibility.)

2. What do you feel are the primary reasons two people should get married? (Answer: God's leading and love.)

Teacher's Note:

Have the class discuss this statement: "Don't look for someone you can live with, look for someone that you can't live without."

Next have them discuss the cartoon on page 112 in the manual. What is the dilemma that the little man is facing? (Answer: Pressure from his grandmother to get married.)

What should be our response to such situations? (Answer: We should be gracious and respectful. They may have very wise insight. In the long run, however, there should be many factors that influence our decision whether or not to marry.)

Principle 2   (DM page 112):

Some people believe marriage will solve their problems.

Teacher's Note:

Clarify that marriage _creates_ a set of problems. That is not bad. It's good. It is through the give-and-take in solving the problems that love is given the opportunity to be tested and to flourish.

Principle 3   (DM page 113):

Many responsibilities are often overlooked.

1. What responsibilities are overlooked?

2. Why do people overlook such crucial items? (Answer: They are often led by their emotions.)

Teacher's Note:

Some other factors that cause young people to rush into marriage are:

1. A lack of willingness to forgo sex. (This is a selfish motivation. It could be damaging to the relationship in the long run.)

2. Teenage pregnancies. (Unfortunately one big mistake often leads to a second big mistake. Counsel from mature, godly people should be sought out in this case.)

VI. According to God, How Far Should You Go Sexually with Your Boy Friend/ Girl Friend?

Illustration: There once was an ad on television trying to sell potato chips. In the ad a person offered an open bag of chips to another person and said, "Bet you can't eat just one." The other person ate one, and, when he tasted how good they were, started shoveling them into his mouth. The drive we have toward sex is much like that. The more you "taste" of sex, the more your appetite grows, and the more you want.

Teacher's Note   (DM page 113):

Discuss each question on this page. The last question hits at the heart of the issue. Use the following verses to discuss it.

Philippians 2:3-4

> Do nothing from selfishness or empty conceit, but with humility of mind let each of you regard one another as more important than himself;
>
> Do not merely look out for your own personal interests, but also for the interests of others.

1. Who should be the most important person in a relationship? (Answer: The other person.)

2. If that is so, what do you communicate to the other person when you constantly challenge him to compromise his principles? (Answer: That you value your needs over his.)

Matthew 26:41

> Keep watching and praying, that you may not enter into temptation; the spirit is willing, but the flesh is weak.

1. What does it mean when it says, "The spirit is willing"? (Answer: You may have every intention of maintaining God's standards, but if you place yourself in tempting or compromising situations often enough, you are likely to succumb to the pressures of the moment.)

2. What do you think Jesus is saying when He says, "Watch and pray"? (Answer: Look out for the situations that are dangerous and pray for the wisdom and strength to avoid them.)

Project B:

To close this discussion on question 6, have the students respond to this statement: Guys give love to get sex, girls give sex to get love. Ask if they agree or disagree. Ask, Why or why not.

VII. Why Are Guys So Sexually Aggressive?

Transparency #44

Key Principles:

1. Guys have strong biological drives.

2. Guys have strong emotional drives.

3. Guys are often motivated by what is the acceptable standard of the world.

4. Some guys don't understand that their aggressive affections mislead the girl and ultimately leave her feeling used.

Teacher's Note:

Each paragraph deals with a different aspect of this problem. As you read each paragraph, have the students isolate the principle.

Principle 1   (DM page 114):

Guys have strong biological drives.

1. If a guy realizes that his drives are at their peak, what can he do to keep them controlled? (Answer: He should first of all be controlled by the Holy Spirit. Second, he should not arrange for situations that tempt him strongly to make sexual advances, e.g., parked cars, prolonged unchaperoned evenings.)

2. What do girls do that makes it harder for guys to control their sexual drives? (Answer: They dress in a provocative manner. Some girls play up to a guy physically. When he suddenly comes on strong, they can't understand. Some are not careful to communicate through their actions that they have boundaries.)

Principle 2   (DM page 114):

Guys have strong emotional drives.

1. Are emotions basically honest or dishonest? (Answer: Although some feel that emotions are neutral, neither right nor wrong, emotions tend to deceive a person. See Jeremiah 17:9.)

2. Do emotions tend to be selfish? (Answer: Yes.)

Teacher's Note:

Since our emotions have a tendency toward dishonesty and selfishness, guys need to realize that what might be _feeling_ so right might not be honoring to God.

Principle 3   (DM page 115):

Guys are often motivated by what is the acceptable standard of the world.

Supplemental Verse:

Romans 12:2

Teacher's Note:

Have your students read the paragraph at the top of page 115 in the manual. Have them discuss the statements from the girl's perspective. How does it feel to be conquered? What does it communicate about the guy's affections? What does it say about his walk with God?

Principle 4   (DM page 115):

Some guys don't understand that their aggressive affections mislead the girl and ultimately leave her feeling used.

Teacher's Note:

Have the class discuss this statement: "Excesses tend to be dangerous." Ask if they agree or disagree. Have them defend their answers. Have them look at Ephesians 5:18. Draw the following formulas on an overhead or chalkboard to make a point.

Excessive physical drives = danger.

Excessive emotional drives = danger.

Excessive peer pressure = danger.

Excessive ignorance of the opposite sex = danger.

Point out that any one excess is dangerous enough. But all four excesses, functioning simultaneously, usually lead to serious problems.

Supplemental Verse:

Colossians 3:17

Personal Application:

Read the paragraph that starts, "What he needs . . . ." Have them meditate on that statement for a minute. If they are dating someone regularly, have them evaluate that person against that statement. Have them answer these questions in their hearts:

1. Am I controlled by the Holy Spirit on my dates?

2. Do I respect my boyfriend/girl friend?

3. Does he/she respect me?

4. Do we strengthen each other?

Closing Prayer:

If they answered no to any of the above, have them silently pray for God's help in overcoming their particular problem. Close after a few minutes of silent prayer.

QUESTIONS ON DATING
Lesson 16

(Discussion Manual pages 115-19)

Introduction:

This would be a good lesson to bring in outside help. You might want to bring in some parents to share their feelings about going steady (question X). A godly woman could discuss understanding girls (question IX). Take advantage of the flexibility of these lessons to use a variety of approaches.

Key Principles:

1. *Some guys are too busy to get involved with girls.*

2. *Some guys are interested in girls but are afraid to initiate a relationship with them.*

3. *Some guys are hesitant to get involved with girls because of unpleasant experiences in the past.*

VIII. *Why Are Some Guys so Afraid to Get Involved with Girls?*

Teacher's Note:

If you are teaching a coeducational class, this question might get more response from the girls. Encourage a lot of participation from everyone.

Principle 1   *(DM page 115):*

Some guys are too busy to get involved with girls.

1. *Do you think that being too busy is a legitimate reason for not getting involved with girls? (Answer: Yes. It is really an individual decision based on individual needs.)*

2. *If a guy chooses not to date girls during his high school years, does that mean he is not socially developed? (Answer: No way. In fact, some social pressures (like dating) can do a lot of damage to a person if one is not prepared for them.)*

Principle 2   *`(DM page 115):*

Some guys are interested in girls but are afraid to initiate a relationship with them.

Teacher's Note:

Have the students list the reasons given in the first paragraph on page 116 for guys being hesitant to show interest in girls. Write them on an overhead or chalkboard. Feel free to expand the list.

Reasons for holding back . . .

· fear of rejection

· fear of having his feelings hurt

· the person is too good-looking to be interested in him

Notice that those feelings can be the same reasons that a girl would hesitate to get involved with a guy.

Principle 3   (DM page 116):

Some guys are hesitant to get involved with girls because of unpleasant experiences in the past.

Teacher's Note:

The important thing is not whether we "get a boyfriend," but whether we *glorify* God in our relationships. We should not feel compelled to date or force a relationship. Put the priority on glorifying God, and let Him lead you from there.

IX. Should You Try to Understand Girls or Just Try to Care for Them the Best You Can?

Teacher's Note:

If you have girls in your class, have them write down some of the things about themselves that they don't think guys understand. Have them turn in their papers. Read some without pointing out who wrote them. You might want to get a godly woman to handle part of this question for you.

Project A:

Divide up the class into small groups and have the students make a list of what they feel are the essential needs of a girl. Have each group share its findings. Compile a complete list of needs. (Make sure they emphasize spiritual needs.) Next have a discussion as to how a guy could meet those needs (either by doing certain things or not doing certain things).

X. What About Going Steady?

Project B:

Have the class develop a Benefits/Liabilities chart on going steady. It should look something like this:

GOING STEADY

Benefits   Liabilities

1.   1.

2.   2.

It is important the the liabilities list be developed honestly. Some suggestions for it would be: (1) limits the amount of friends of the opposite sex that you have, (2) puts a heavier emotional burden on the couple, (3) because of their familiarity, it raises the level of temptation toward sexual sin, (4) has a way of making you feel trapped, and (5) we tend to put the person we're going with ahead of the Lord, our family, and our friends. Open up the class discussion on this subject.

Teacher's Note:

Discuss the subject of parents. Take a poll to see how many of your students' parents are in favor or not in favor of going steady. Discuss the reasons that they've given their children for their position on going steady. Next discuss alternatives to going steady.

1. Is going steady the only way to demonstrate a special admiration for a guy or girl? (Answer: No. Treating them special will communicate more in the long run than giving a class ring.)

2. What are some ways you can get to know guys/girls without locking yourself into long-term commitments? (Answer: Date around, go to a lot of social activities in groups, put emphasis on spiritual gatherings like youth group.)

XI. What About Kissing on the First Date?

Teacher's Note:

Poll the class on the following questions.

1. How many think that it's all right to kiss on the first date?

2. How many feel that it's not all right?

3. What do you desire to communicate by kissing your date?

4. What do you see as the liabilities of kissing your date the first time you go out?

5. We often have a selfish motive when we kiss our dates. We aren't so much giving something as taking something. Do you agree or disagree?

Supplemental Verse:

Colossians 3:17

According to this verse, we should ask ourselves if Jesus Christ's reputation will be built up or brought down by our sexual behavior on the first date or any date.

XII. What Are Some of the Needs Girls Have That I Can Meet?

Transparency #45

Key Principles:

1. Christian girls need to have their relationships with Christ developed.

2. Girls need to feel accepted for who they are.

3. Girls need to have meaningful conversations.

Teacher's Note:

This is obviously not an exhaustive list. Look again at the lists your students made for the project on question IX. Compare it to the three areas listed on pages 118-19. If you left out any of those items, list them now. This will serve as a review for your students.

Principle 1

Christian girls need to have their relationships with Christ developed.

Besides meeting an immediate need for the girl and guy, what other benefits could come from concentrating on spiritual things while on a date? (Answer: The couple would present a good example to other Christian couples. The couple would be less likely to fall into sexual sin.)

> Warning: Don't think that because you pray or read the Bible together that you can't fall into sexual sin. Satan wants us to think that we're safe in order to catch us off guard. Remember Matthew 26:41.

Principle 2:

Girls need to feel accepted for who they are.

1. What does the author mean when he speaks of a "performance basis" relationship? (Answer: It means a person has to meet a standard imposed on them by someone else.)

2. What are some of the problems with a performance-based love? (Answer: The person does not always know what is expected of them. The person isn't always capable of meeting the standard. It makes the person feel that he is not good enough as he is.)

3. What does Romans 5:8 say about how Christ responded to us? (Answer: He accepted us even though we were sinners.)

4. How should Christ's attitude toward us affect our attitude toward people we date? (Answer: We should accept them with their strengths and their weaknesses. Accepting a fault does not mean that we aren't to try to help them better themselves. It simply means that our love for them will remain in spite of shortcomings.)

Principle 3:

Girls need to have meaningful conversations.

Teacher's Note:

Read the first paragraph in this section. Include a statement about the importance of listening. Meaningful conversation requires that we listen closely to one another. One of the benefits of meaningful conversation is that you get to know each other's interests, fears, joys, and convictions. This takes a relationship beyond a superficial level. It also gives the couple a better position to evaluate each other as potential marriage partners.

Personal Application:

Suggest that each student decide on a specific time this week to have an in-depth conversation with the person he or she is dating. Have them think of things they do not know about their boy/girl friends (likes, dislikes, opinions, etc.) and encourage them to ask about those things.

Closing Prayer:

Remind the students that there will be one more lesson dealing with questions on dating. Close in prayer, emphasizing their need to be committed to God in their dating lives.

QUESTIONS ON DATING
Lesson 17

(Discussion Manual pages 119-23)

Teacher's Note:

This lesson deals with extremely delicate topics. Questions 16 and 17 talk about what to do if you've already gone too far. Depending on the size and gender of your class, you may want to handle these questions yourself with the lecture method of teaching. A question directed at an individual might be interpreted wrong. Although the lesson plan will look the same as other lessons, you may choose to answer the questions yourself.

Introduction:

Briefly discuss how their dating lives have been going. If they are not dating, take a few minutes for "small talk" to get to know them better. Open in prayer, asking God for help as you look once again at this important subject. Thank Him for the guidelines that set us free to enjoy ourselves.

Key Principles:

1. *Physical activity can hamper your desire to communicate with one another.*

2. *Heavy sexual involvement takes the focus off the person's needs.*

3. *Physical involvement can be misinterpreted by the girl to be love.*

XIII. *Is There Any Way That Sex Strengthens a Dating Relationship?*

Teacher's Note   *(DM page 119):*

You should notice that all three answers given in the manual point to the negative effects of sex on a relationship. Sex is wonderful <u>for</u> <u>marriage</u>, but it weakens the fiber of a relationship prior to marriage. This should be emphasized at the outset. Have a student read the first paragraph under question 13.

Supplemental Verses:

1 Corinthians 6:18-20

> *Flee immorality. Every other sin that a man commits is outside the body, but the immoral man sins against his own body.*
>
> *Or do you not know that your body is a temple of the Holy Spirit who is in you, whom you have from God, and that you are not your own?*
>
> *For you have been bought with a price: therefore glorify God in your body.*

1. According to these verses, does premarital sex strengthen a relationship? (Answer: No, it destroys the whole person.)

2. Do we have the right to abuse our bodies? (Answer: No. Our bodies belong to God.)

Principle 1   (DM page 119):

Physical activity can hamper your desire to communicate with each other.

1. How does guilt destroy communication? (Answer: It lowers your attitude of yourself. It mars your fellowship with God, thereby breaking down communication with Him. It makes discussing anything of importance irrelevant, since there is such a large hurt in your heart and your relationship.)

2. If you don't have adequate communication in a relationship, what hope is there for you? (Answer: None.)

Transition:

A heavy sexual involvement in a relationship brings on guilt. Guilt breaks down the communication in the relationship. Unfortunately, unless the couple is willing to stop their sexual involvement, they usually get even more heavily involved sexually. This leads to another problem in the relationship.

Principle 2   (DM page 120):

Heavy sexual involvement takes the focus off of the person's needs.

Read the first paragraph at the top of the page.

1. What does a girl mean when she says she feels like an object? (Answer: She feels that her guy is only seeing her for what he gets from her.)

2. How can this deteriorate love? (Answer: Love wants to give, lust wants to get. 1 Corinthains 13:5 says that love "does not seek its own".)

Principle 3   (DM page 120):

Physical involvement can be misinterpreted by the girl to be love.

Teacher's Note:

Have someone read paragraph 2 on page 120 out loud. End the discussion on this question by giving some advice. The best way to know whether or not your relationship is being held together by sexual involvement is to stop the sexual *involvement. If the guy will accept you only if you give him what he wants, you have no love relationship. You have only a sexual relationship. God is not pleased with this, and you probably aren't, either.*

XIV. How Do You Turn a Guy Down Without Hurting Him and Still Remain His Friend?

Supplemental Verses:

Ephesians 4:25,32

Teacher's Note:

Use the supplemental verses to emphasize the importance of honesty and kindness. You should qualify this question by mentioning that in most cases, it is impossible not to hurt a guy when turning him down. He is going to be disappointed. The important thing is that the girl rejects the <u>request</u>, not the guy.

XV. I See a Lot of Beautiful, Sexy Women Every Day. Is Simply Looking at Them Lusting?

Teacher's Note:

Clarify that guys are not the only people with a lusting problem. Girls can also be guilty of mentally undressing a guy and imagining a sexual relationship with him.

Key Verses:

Matthew 5:27-28

1. *Why does God consider looking at a woman with sexual thoughts as bad as really committing sexual sins with her? (Answer: Because we are always judged on our actions <u>and</u> our attitudes.)*

2. *If I am guilty of committing intercourse by thinking it, why not just do the real thing? God is going to be displeased anyway. (Answer: 1 If you commit adultery after lusting, you're guilty twice.   2 You also cause the girl to be disobedient to God.)*

Teacher's Note:

God considers lusting dangerous because it is polluting our minds. God wants our minds to be pure.

Supplemental Verse:

Romans 12:2

1. Is lusting a way that we conform to the world? (Answer: Yes.)

2. How can we know that a thought is renewing our minds? (Answer: The thought will be good, acceptable, or perfect.)

3. Why is lusting so harmful to us? (Answer: It takes our minds off of holy thoughts. It lowers our view of the opposite sex from people to objects. It feeds our selfish natures.)

Teacher's Note:

Go over the three stages of lusting. Stop here and lead the class in prayer. Ask God to give each one a desire to keep his mind pure and to honor God by only viewing members of the opposite sex in respectful ways.

Next formulate a few suggestions to help overcome lusting. Ask the students for suggestions. Here are a few that should provide help.

1. Don't look at girls or guys deliberately to lust after them (Job 31:1).

2. Remove stimuli that cause you to think about sex more often (pornography, sexual books and movies, sexually explicit music).

3. Pray daily for God to fill your mind.

4. When confronted by an attractive member of the opposite sex:

   Acknowledge his/her attractiveness.

   Thank God for making him attractive.

   Ask yourself the question, "I wonder if he/she knows the Lord. (This puts your focus on his real need, not your selfish need.)

XVI. We Didn't plan to, but My boyfriend and I Have Gone Too Far. How Did We Get into This Situation?

Teacher's Note:

Read the first paragraph on page 122 in the manual and read through the chart. Share the following principles designed to keep them safe from sexual sins.

Remember that:

1. *Sex has a constant appetite. If you feed it a little, it just wants more. (So don't start feeding it.)*

2. *The closer you get to intercourse, the harder it is to go back to just holding hands.*

3. *The best policy is to determine in advance that you are not going to step beyond the first or second level. Inform a date or boyfriend/girl friend whenever you sense them testing your limits.*

4. *Avoid situations that make it easier to fall into sin (parked cars, unchaperoned times at your homes, etc.)*

5. *Admit when you feel your emotions getting the best of you. Pray immediately and ask God to intervene.*

6. *If a dating partner persists in pushing you beyond your limits, don't date him/her anymore.*

7. *If possible, confide in your parents or trusted older friend if you feel your emotions are controlling you too much.*

XVII. If My Girlfriend and I Have Gone Too Far, What Are Some Positive Steps We Can Take to Resolve the Situation?

Teacher's Note:

Do not encourage dialogue for this part of the lesson. Do straight teaching. It would be best to have your principles written out on a transparency or poster in advance. The following material is provided to augment what is in the manual.

1. *Talk together about your sexual problem.*

   a. *If one person is not willing to <u>admit</u> that you have a problem, it's probably time to break up.*

   b. *Acknowledge the feelings of guilt.*

   c. *If necessary, talk your problem over with your pastor, youth pastor, or trustworthy friend.*

2. *Agree together that you sinned against God and each other.*

   a. *If one tries to justify your actions, it is evident that that person wants to continue having sexual intercourse in defiance of God. In that case, it's probably time to break up.*

   b. *Confess your sin to God and ask Him to forgive you.*

   c. *Realize that God will indeed forgive you. He does not want you carrying a load of guilt that He has already paid for.*

    d.   Commit to God and to each other a willingness to do <u>whatever</u> is necessary to insure that you don't have this problem again.

    e.   Be willing to seek reliable counsel if you either continue to feel guilty or continue to have sexual problems.

3. Plan dates that maximize fun and common interests but minimize sexual temptation.

    a.   If you have fallen into intercourse once, it's very easy to fall again. You figure that you've already lost your virginity, so what's the use? Therefore, plan dates that will not grant you the opportunities to be alone for a long period of time.

    b.   Go on double dates.

    c.   Don't stay out when you don't have something meaningful or planned to do.

    d.   Spend more of your dates doing activities with your youth group or Christian friends.

4. Commit your evening to the Lord in prayer.

    a.   Don't ever deny your potential to sin.

    b.   Spend time talking about your love for God and His love for you.

    c.   Visualize Christ's sacrifice for you when you are tempted to sin. His love will give you strength.

    d.   Pray whenever you feel your emotions getting the best of you.

5. Decide together to break up if you can't resist sexual temptation.

Supplemental Verses:

Matthew 18:7-9

Jesus is saying that we should do whatever is necessary to remove stumbling blocks to our relationship with Him. If it means losing something very important to us, like a boyfriend or girl friend, He says it's worth it in the long run.

Personal Application:

Encourage your students to seek responsible help or advice if they are having problems in any area of their dating or sexual lives.

Closing Prayer:

Thank God for His wonderful gift of sexual love. Ask Him to help your students preserve His gift unblemished until they are free to experience it to the maximum within the safety of marriage.

PEER PRESSURE
Lesson 18

(Discussion Manual pages 125-35)

Introduction:

The next three lessons deal with one of the most menacing problems to young people today. All young people, without exception, fight the battle of being influenced by the crowd that they hang around with. Fortunately, the Bible has much to say on this subject. This lesson will discuss the definition of peer pressure, and how to resist it.

Have your students offer their definitions of peer pressure. Have them share examples of it at their school.

Key Principles:

1. We need to know what peer pressure is.

2. We need to know how to resist peer pressure.

I. What is Peer Pressure?

Principle 1   (DM page 126):

We need to know what peer pressure is.

Transparency #46

Teacher's Note:

The first paragraph on this page defines what peer pressure is. Have a student read the definition out loud. Ask the students for examples of good peer pressure. (The influence that a committed Christian has on his friends would be an example of good peer pressure.)

Supplemental Verses:

Exodus 32:1-6,19-24

1. Why did Aaron make the golden calf? (Answer: The crowd was pressuring him into giving them a god.)

2. Did Aaron know better than to submit to those people? (Answer: Yes.)

3. Why do you think Aaron gave in to their demands? (Answer: He was afraid of what it would cost him to stand for his convictions.)

Teacher's Note   *(DM page 126):*

The second paragraph on this page tells *why* peer pressure influences young people so much. It can be summed up in one word--rejection. Have the students go down the list at the bottom of the page. Have them tell how fear of rejection can cause them to be manipulated in some of those areas.

Transparency #47

1. What is a chameleon? (Answer: a lizard that changes colors to whatever his surroundings are in order to go undetected.)

2. How does the behavior of a chameleon resemble a Christian's submitting to peer pressure? (Answer: A Christian giving in to the demands of the crowd is not wanting to be known as a Christian for fear of rejection.)

3. How do you think God feels when we do that?

4. What does that say about our love for God? (Answer: At times it isn't as great as our love for the crowd.)

Transition:

None of us is immune to the pressures of the crowd. We all want to be loved and accepted. But too often the price we have to pay is just too expensive. No popularity or acceptance is worth compromising our convictions.

II. How Do I Resist Peer Pressure?

Principle 2   *(DM page 127):*

We need to learn how to resist peer pressure.

Teacher's Note:

Ask your students for their definition of "worldly." Compare theirs with the definition at the top of page 128 in the manual.

Transparency #48

Key Verses:

1 John 2:15-17

Teacher's Note:

Have your students respond to the questions on page 128. Emphasize that God does not like sharing us with Satan. When we love the things that are contrary to God's nature, we are really saying that we don't care about God very much.

Supplemental Verse:

Luke 16:13

1. According to this verse, can we be devoted to two masters at the same time? (Answer: No.)

2. Why? (Answer: Because we will naturally be loyal to one master at the expense of the other.)

Teacher's Note:

Make a chart that will consolidate the materials covered on pages 129-34 in the manual. Fill it out as you come to the material. It should include the following information:

Transparency #49

1. Lust of the flesh (DM pages 129-30):

Read the definition on page 129. Begin filling out your chart. Have different students read the examples of the lust of the flesh. After each example have each student rate on a scale of 1 to 10 the severity of the pressure on him to conform (1=very little pressure, 10=extreme pressure). Have them write the number next to each example.

2. Lust of the eyes (DM pages 130-32):

Follow the same procedure as you did for the lust of the flesh. Fill out your chart, read each example, and rate the severity.

1. In the cartoon on page 131, what examples of the lust of the eyes are depicted? (Answer: Big shiny car, telephone in car, fancy clothes and shoes, expensive jewelry on neck and fingers.)

2. What has the little man done to God in his life? (Answer: He shut Him out in favor of things.)

3. When he dies, how many of those neat things does he take with him? (Answer: None.)

4. Is God against our having nice things? (Answer: No. He's against us having things that are more important to us than Him.)

Transparency #51

3. Boastful pride of life (DM pages 132-34):

Follow the same instructions as you did on the lust of the flesh and eyes. Read Philippians 2:3-4.

1. According to verse 3, what motivates a person caught up in the boastful pride of life? (Answer: Selfishness and empty conceit.)

2. What should be our attitude toward others? (Answer: We should see their needs as more important than our own.)

Teacher's Note:

Review your completed chart.

Personal Application: (DM page 135):

Assign specific students to administer the "Will You Remember or Care" inventory to their parents. Tell them to bring back their results next lesson to share with the class. You should give them a reminder call on this assignment a couple of days before the next lesson. Also, have each student go back over the examples of peer pressure that he rated on a scale of 1-10. Have the students make a list of them from the one in which he feels the most pressure to conform to the one in which he feels the least pressure to conform.

Give a few minutes for them to silently pray about the three most severe areas that they have. Encourage them to acknowledge those areas to God, to ask His forgiveness for the times they have given in to the world's pressures, and ask for God's help in resisting the world in those areas.

Closing Prayer:

Remind the students that God wants us to love people and use things. The world wants us to love things and use people. Read Romans 12:2. Close in prayer.

PEER PRESSURE
Lesson 19

(Discussion Manual pages 136-41)

Introduction:

Reproduce the chart from the last lesson on a poster or an overhead transparency. Briefly review the definition of peer pressure and the contents of the chart. (Save this chart. You will use it next lesson also.) Have the students to whom you assigned the "Will You Remember or Care" inventory share their findings. There may be only a few questions that their parents will be able to answer. In light of the test results, ask the following questions:

1. *How important do the items on the test seem now as those parents looked back?*

2. *What bearing do any of the items on the test have on today?*

3. *What lesson do we learn from the test results? (Answer: It is silly to be manipulated by peer pressure.)*

4. *What is important in life? Why? (Answer: What we do about and for Jesus Christ, because He is eternal, and how we respond to Him affects our eternal destiny.)*

Transition:

If we choose to live for Jesus Christ rather than submit to the crowd, we must be prepared to deal with the consequences. The consequences of not submitting to peer group pressure often include being misunderstood, disliked, and unwelcome.

III. Another Way for a Christian Student to Overcome Peer Pressure

Key Principles:

1. *We need to realize that we might not win a popularity contest on our campus for living for Jesus Christ.*

2. *We need to realize when people reject us for our walk with God, they are really rejecting Jesus Christ.*

3. *We need to realize that Christ wants us to be very happy when we are rejected by others because of Him.*

Principle 1   *(DM page 136):*

We need to realize that we might not win a popularity contest on our campus for living for Jesus Christ.

91

Transparency #52

Teacher's Note:

Have students describe some of the reactions they or their friends have received because they chose to resist peer pressure and stand for God.

Transparency #53

Key Verse:

2 Timothy 3:12

Supplemental Verses:

Joshua 24:14-15

1. According to 2 Timothy 3:12, is persecution a sign of godliness? (Answer: No, persecution is a <u>result</u> of godly living--not a sign of it.)

2. Why is that distinction important? (Answer: We may also be persecuted because we are weird or obnoxious. That is not pleasing to God.)

3. Would it be fair to say, however, that if we are <u>not</u> experiencing any kind of persecution that we may not be standing out as a godly person? (Answer: Yes, that's a fair conclusion.)

Key Verses:

John 17:14-15

Project:

"Neighbor-Nudging." Have each person pair up with a neighbor to discuss the following:

1. I recently felt persecuted for my faith when I--

2. In situations like this, I usually respond by--

3. When I need encouragement for my testimony on campus, I go to--

Allow two minutes.

Principle 2   (DM page 138):

We need to realize when people reject us for our walk with God, they are really rejecting Jesus Christ.

Illustration: *A policeman represents the law. When he writes a person a ticket because his radar said that person was speeding, he may take some verbal abuse. He may in some cases risk physical abuse. But it is his responsibility to represent the law, and taking abuse goes with that responsibility. I doubt seriously if he goes back to his car after issuing a ticket and cries because someone called him a name. They may appear angry at the officer as the law's representative, but in reality they are mad at the law for disciplining them.*

Key Verses:

John 15:19-20

If "a slave is not greater than his master," do we have the right to expect different or better treatment than Christ received? (Answer: No.)

Transparency #54

Teacher's Note:

Read the paragraph at the top of page 139 in the manual.

Key Verses:

John 3:19-20

Illustration: When murderers or thieves are depicted in movies, they usually want to do their dirty deeds in the dark. In a typical scene a person carrying a light might suddenly come upon them--exposing their deeds. Their normal reaction is to do whatever is necessary to eliminate the light. Sometimes that involves hurting or eliminating the <u>person</u> *carrying the light. We carry the light of God's truth. We can be certain that the more we flash His truth around sinful people, the more they will attack us for carrying the light.*

Principle 3   *(DM page 140);*

We need to realize Christ wants us to be very happy when we are rejected by others because of Him.

Transparency #55

Key Verses:

Matthew 5:10-12

Teacher's Note:

Jesus is not saying that we should go out and throw a party every time we get insulted or assaulted for our faith. He realizes that we can be hurt. What He is saying in this passage is that we should be happy because:

1. *That is the price of being a member of His Kingdom.*

2. *We will be rewarded by God for our faithfulness. (His reward will far outweigh our suffering.)*

3. *We identify with millions of faithful men and women who have boldly stood up for His name.*

We also identify with the Lord Himself. It is a privilege to be counted worthy to suffer for Him (1 Peter 2:21).

Key Verses:

Acts 5:40-41

Personal Application:

Using the three Key Principles, have the students write a letter to Jesus. Have them: (1) ask God for help enduring the rejection they sometimes feel, (2) mention a person they believe has reacted to God's Spirit in their testimony, and (3) thank God for being allowed to suffer for Him.

Encourage the students to be sensitive to the peer pressure they experience this week. Suggest that they take their letters to God with them and read them whenever they are experiencing strong pressure.

Closing Prayer:

When they are finished with their letters, have them read the letters back to God as a closing prayer.

PEER PRESSURE
Lesson 20

(Discussion Manual pages 142-46)

Introduction:

Highlight the first lesson (lesson 18) by defining peer pressure (DM page 126) and by using the chart that you developed from that lesson. Review the second lesson (lesson 19) by going over the three Key Prinicples. In the first lesson we discussed how to respond to the pressure. In the second lesson we discussed how we should respond to the consequences of overcoming the pressure. This lesson we are going to discuss how to respond to the people who lash out at us. We are going to look at them from God's perspective.

Key Principles:

1. Man is small and weak in God's eyes.

2. God sees man through the eyes of compassion.

3. God sees man with an eternal perspective.

Transparencys #56 — #57

Teacher's Note: *(DM page 142):*

Briefly discuss the cartoons on this page. Have the students comment on what they mean.

1. What is the danger of looking at the "stars" of this world from a human perspective? (Answer: We can develop a fear of them, which would cause us to dislike them.)

2. What is the benefit of looking at the stars of this world from a divine perspective? (Answer: We can see them for what they really are and love them.)

Principle 1   *(DM page 143):*

Man is small and weak in God's eyes.

Teacher's Note:

One of your students may ask how God could say He is interested in man if indeed we are as insignificant as a drop in the bucket. Acknowledge his insight and point out that you will cover that next. That could cloud the impact of this Key Principle if it were answered now. Your students need to see that they do not need to fear anyone who threatens them for their faith.

Key Verses:

Isaiah 40:15-17

Teacher's Note:

To support these verses, you may want to go over the story of the twelve spies sent out at Kadesh-barnea (Numbers 13:1-33). Ten spies looked at the Caananites as "giants" that made them feel like grasshoppers. But Joshua and Caleb looked at the giants from God's perspective. They feared neither their size nor their power because they knew that they were like dust in the hands of God. Pursue this only if time permits.

Project   (DM page 143):

Follow the instructions at the bottom of the page, except for this one modification: Have the students name people from current events or politics that are abusing people. World leaders who oppress their people or hardened criminals will meet the requirements. Insert their names in the blanks of Psalm 146:3-4. We make this suggestion since, in a class situation, some of the people that they name from school might be friends with other students in your class.

Next have them think of the one person that intimidates them most at school. Have them repeat the following prayer after you, inserting the person's name silently.

> Dear Father, Thank You for being greater than all men put together. Forgive me for fearing _____.
> As long as I fear _____, I can't show Your love to him/her. Enable me this week to love _____ no matter what might happen to me. I thank You that ultimately I will be victorious for obeying You. Amen.

Transition:

If we only saw man as being unimportant in God's eyes, we might think that God is not interested in him. But the truth is that man, as puny as he is in God's eyes, is the focus of His interest. With that in mind, let's look at the second principle.

Principle 2   (DM page 144):

God sees man through the eyes of compassion.

Transparency #58

Teacher's Note:

Read the first paragraph on this page out loud.

Key Verse:

Matthew 9:36

> 1. *Why did Jesus feel compassion for the crowd? (Answer: Because they were troubled, depressed, and aimlessly lost.)*
>
> 2. *Should we expect kind and rational treatment from people who are hurting and lost? (Answer: No. Often their harsh response to our faith is a test to see if it's real. If we stand firm, it might be the first time they have seen anyone with a purpose for living.)*

Supplemental Verses:

Luke 23:34

Jesus was able to have love and pity for His murderers. Remember--we were His murderers!

Acts 7:54-60

Stephen was able to have love and pity for his murderers because he was aware of God's presence and strength in his life.

Transition:

God does not want us to fear our enemies, because He has ultimate control. He wants us to love them just as He loved us. There is one more principle we need as we overcome the grip of peer pressure in our lives.

Principle 3   *(DM page 145):*

God sees man from an eternal perspective.

Transparency #59

Teacher's Note:

Have the students comment about the cartoon on page 145 in the Discussion Manual. Make sure they understand that we exist in a small little speck of time, which does not threaten an infinite God. All of the things that man desires--the lust of the flesh, the lust of the eyes, and the boastful pride of life--are temporary. When it comes down to what really matters, none of those things have any importance.

Key Verses:

Psalm 37:1-5

Personal Application:

Have your students answer the questions on page 146 in their manuals. Go back over them, asking students to volunteer their answers.

Repeat the three Key Principles. Then read "In Conclusion" on page 146 as a summary of all of the thoughts of this chapter. Close with the proverb "Only one life, t'will soon be past. Only what's done for Christ will last."

Closing Prayer.

MAKING FRIENDS
Lesson 21

(Discussion Manual pages 149-60)

Introduction:

Teacher, the next three lessons deal with the importance of friendship. All people, of all ages, need friends. But the friends that we have through our high school years play an extremely significant role in the building of our character and self-image. Therefore, these lessons may be a strategic time of learning and evaluation. Be sensitive to those students who may have the wrong kind of friends, or may not have any genuine friends at all. Pray that your time spent together on this subject may bring about a change in their lives.

This lesson covers sections I and II in the Discussion Manual. There is more material here than you will probably have time to cover. Ask for God's guidance as you choose the material best suited for your students.

Key Principles:

1. Friends can be a source of encouragement for us--as well as we can to them.

2. Friends can give difficult, but needed, counsel for our lives--and we can do the same for them.

3. Friends can see potential in us, and we in them, which we may not be able to see ourselves.

4. God wants us to make sure that we choose the right kind of friends.

5. God wants us to be the kind of friends who have great understanding.

6. God wants us to be the kind of friends who are trustworthy.

7. God wants us to be the kind of friends who will not hold a grudge.

Project A:

Pass out 3"x5" cards to the students. Have them write out the names of their three closest friends. (This will be the first of two self-evaluation quizzes they will take.) Have them answer the following questions:

1. Do these people know that I consider them my closest friends?

2. Have I been as good a friend to them as I am capable of being?

3. Am I willing to be open to God's showing me how to improve my friendship?

Lead them in prayer, asking God to teach you all through this lesson, to be better friends to those who are counting on you.

I. The Importance of Friends

Principle 1   (DM page 151):

Friends can be a source of encouragement for us--as well as we can for them.

Transparency #60

Key Verses:

Ecclesiastes 4:9-11

Teacher's Note:

Have the students answer the questions to this passage. Follow with this think question (no verbal answer is necessary).

1. Have any of my friends been discouraged lately?

2. Did I go out of my way to assure them of my love and encourage them?

Key Verse: (DM page 152);

Proverbs 17:77 (answer the questions).

Transition:

Friends are great to have when you are discouraged. They can build you up just when you think life is getting the best of you. Sometimes, however, a friend is called on to be the _cause_ of difficult feelings by giving you honest critique. That is brought out in our next principle.

Principle 2   (DM page 152):

Friends can give difficult, but needed, counsel for our lives, and we can do the same for them.

Teacher's Note:

Accountability is one of the missing ingredients in many friendships. We are willing to listen to the advice or counsel of a friend until it conflicts with our desires. But the wise person is one who does not assume he is beyond rebuke or counsel.

Supplemental Verses:

Proverbs 12:15; 20:18; 27:9

1. *Do you feel that your friends are free to critique you?*

2. *How would they answer that question?*

3. *When was the last time a friend gave you advice or counsel that was difficult to accept?*

4. *How did you respond to it?*

5. *Have I been faithful enough to my friends to tell them what they need to hear?*

Principle 3   *(DM page 153):*

Friends can see potential in us, and we in them, which we may not be able to see ourselves.

Key Verse:

1 Timothy 4:12

Project B:

Have them take out the 3"x5" cards that they used at the beginning.   Remind them of the three Key Principles. Have them respond to these questions:

1. *If I am going to take this lesson seriously, I need to--*

2. *One specific area I need to change in friendships is --*

3. *This is what I'm going to do this week to improve this area of my friendships.*

Give them a moment to pray, asking God for strength to follow through with this action.

Transition:

Friends play a key role in our walk with God. God wants us to have the right kind of friends and to be the right kind of friends. The next four principles will show us ways that we can improve our walk with God by improving the kind of friends that we have--and the kind of friends we are.

II. What Qualities Does God Want Us to Choose in Our Friends?

Principle 4   *(DM page 154):*

God wants us to make sure that we choose the right kind of friends.

Key Verse:

Proverbs 27:19

    1. What characteristics of mine do I see reflected in my friends?

    2. What characteristics of my friends do I see reflected in me?

    3. Are those characteristics good?

Teacher's Note:

Have the students complete the list of negative effects on this page.

Key Verse:

1 Corinthians 15:33

    1. Is my relationship with God improving as a result of my friends' influence?

    2. Is their relationship with God improving because of my influence?

    3. Have I given my non-Christian friends a positive view of a Christian?

    4. How have my friends affected my attitude toward my parents? My schoolwork? My casual friends?

Teacher's Note:

You should challenge your students to seriously reconsider their close friends if those friends are a negative influence on their Christian walk. It is better to lose a friend than to lose a good testimony for Jesus Christ.

Principle 5   (DM page 155):

God wants us to be the kind of friend who has great understanding.

Transparency #61

Teacher's Note:

Jesus and Peter were great friends. Yet Peter denied three times that He even knew Jesus. Jesus gently showed Peter that He still loved him and that their friendship was as strong as ever. If time permits, relate the background of this story and how Jesus identified with Peter's sorrow in John 21:15-17. He asked Peter three times if he loved Him. This reminder of his denial of Christ at the trial was also a reassurance of Christ's love and confidence in Peter.

Key Verses:

Romans 12:10,15

1. Do you enjoy honoring your friends?

2. In what specific ways do you build up your friends?

Teacher's Note:

Cover the material on page 156 in the manual and have students answer the question at the bottom.

Principle 6   (DM page 157):

God wants us to be the kind of friend who is trustworthy.

Transparency #62

Teacher's Note:

It is important that a friend be trustworthy. That is what distinguishes a friend from any other person in your life. Write out the four characteristics of a trustworthy friend on an overhead or chalkboard. Have them answer the two questions at the bottom of page 158 in their manuals with those four characteristics in mind.

Project C:

Analyze the following situations in light of the four characteristics of a trustworthy friend.

1. Your best friend is driving the school homecoming queen home from their date when, through negligence, he pulls into oncoming traffic. From the accident that occurs, his date receives cuts to her face that radically mar her beauty. What is your response?

2. You are shopping with your girl friend when she puts some jewelry into her purse and walks out of the store. She is caught by store security outside the premises. What is your response?

(Teacher, feel free to make up situations that best fit your students.)

Does standing up for a friend mean that we defend them when they are obviously guilty? (Answer: No. We stick up for them when we feel they are being misjudged. We stand beside them when they are bearing the consequences of their guilt.)

Principle 7   (DM page 159):

God wants us to be the kind of friends who will not hold a grudge.

Transparency #63

Key Verses:

Proverbs 22:24-25

> 1. *Have you vented your anger around your friends lately?*
>
> 2. *Have you vented your anger on your friends lately?*

Teacher's Note:

Advise them that they should ask forgiveness of their friends for losing their temper around them or on them.

Key Verse:

Hebrews 12:15

Teacher's Note:

Encourage your students to be honest with themselves regarding grudges. Grudges are like cancer--they slowly eat away at you and are capable of completely destroying your relationships, not to mention your personal happiness.

Personal Application:

Review the seven principles from this lesson. Challenge them to begin applying those principles to their friendships this week.

Closing Prayer:

For the closing prayer, have each student pray silently for the three people on his or her list. Have them thank God for them and ask Him for special help this week as they demonstrate His love to their friends by applying the principles they have just learned.

MAKING FRIENDS
Lesson 22

(Discussion Manual pages 160-67)

Introduction:

Write the seven principles from the last lesson on a poster. Review them for the class. Next, spend a few minutes finding out how students' friendships have been this week. Ask if they were able to use any of the principles from the last lesson.

This lesson is devoted to developing and improving better friendships. There is a lot of practical advice given in the Discussion Manual. The thrust of this lesson is how to take a person from being a stranger to an intimate friend.

III. Everyone Wants Friends--The Problem Is, We Don't Know How To Make Good Friends.

Key Principles:

1. We need to take the initiative to meet and get to know new people in order to better meet their needs.

2. We need to develop closer relationships with casual friends in order to better meet their needs.

3. We need to develop intimate relationships with a few friends in order to better meet their needs.

Principle 1 (DM page 160):

We need to take the initiative to meet and get to know new people in order to better meet their needs.

Teacher's Note:

Give each student a piece of paper. Have each write down the name or some description of a person that he has recently noticed. This should be a person that he would like to get to know as a friend. He will be applying the teaching in this principle to this person.

Have each student go down the list of questions at the top of page 161 in the manual with that person in mind.

Key Verse:

Galatians 6:10

1. What does Paul mean when he says "especially of the household of faith"? (Answer: We should put a priority on making friends among the Christian community.)

2. What person(s) within my church could I get to know (name or description)? Teacher, encourage them to put this principle to work today.

Teacher's Note:

Have each pray for the courage this week to initiate a friendship with the person he picked out at the beginning of the lesson.

Transition:

Noticing potential friends around us is important. But they will remain strangers unless we break the ice by striking up conversations with them. The next material we look at will give us guidelines for initiating conversation.

Teacher's Note:

Teach straight from page 162 of the Discussion Manual. Go over each step with them. Allow them to ask any questions of clarification.

Project:

"Game Plan." Have each student write out a game plan for getting to know the person they isolated at the beginning of the lesson. They should answer the following questions:

1. When am I going to meet him (day and time)?

2. Where am I going to meet him (be specific)?

3. What leading question am I going to use to begin the conversation?

4. What things do we have in common that I could use to talk about (same third period class, mutual friend, etc.)?

Pray for them to carry out their Game Plans this week. Tell them to be prepared to report back next week on how their first contacts went.

Principle 2   (DM page 163):

We need to develop closer relationships with casual friends in order to better meet their needs.

Teacher's Note:

On another piece of paper each will write the name of a casual friend he would like to know better. Encourage choosing a person who is a Christian since that person could develop into an intimate friend later on.

Supportive Precept 1:

You must begin to pray about this person and his needs.

    1. What are this person's most urgent needs?

    2. In what ways can I help meet those needs?

Teacher's Note:

Have each pray right now for that person and his or her needs.

Supportive Precept 2:

You must be sincere about who you are and the needs you have.

    1. Does this person have a realistic idea of my strengths and weaknesses?

    2. What needs do I have that this person could help meet? (Remind the students that it would not be fair to deprive their friends of the privilege of helping them. It's great to be needed.)

Supportive Precept 3:

We must be willing to learn about the deep desires and dreams of our friends.

    1. What dreams and desires do I know that he/she has?

    2. When could I spend some time with him in the next week to learn more about his dreams and desires?

Supportive Precept 4:

We must be willing to become sensitive to spiritual strengths and weaknesses.

    1. With my present knowledge, what would I say is my friend's greatest spiritual strength? Weakness?

    2. How could I be more sensitive to those specific needs?

Supportive Precept 5:

We must continue to take the initiative to be a friend.

    1. What could I invite this person to do with me in order to enhance our friendship?

    2. When will I ask this friend to that event?

Transition:

Making friends helps us meet more people's needs. Getting to know some friends better helps us meet their particular needs better. But sometimes we need more than _just_ a friend. We need to have a few intimate friends for whom we are willing give whatever is necessary to build them up.

Principle 3   (DM page 165):

We need to develop intimate relationships with a few friends in order to better meet their needs.

Teacher's Note:

Most high school students want to be close to two or three people (and many are). It is difficult to have more than three intimate friends, as the drain on their emotions becomes too great. On one more piece of paper, each should write the name of a friend that he wants to become an intimate friend. (This is to be a person of the same gender!) He is to keep this person in mind as you go over the four supportive precepts.

Transparency #64

Supportive Precept 1:

Intimate friends must be open to having deep joys and deep pain.

    1. Am I willing to share my pains with this person?

    2. Am I willing to give of myself to suffer with him through deep pain?

    3. What deep joy or pain am I experiencing right now that I should share with this friend?

Key Verses:

Psalm 55:12-14

Transparency #65

Supportive Precept 2:

Intimate friends must be willing to stand by and bear the burdens, sorrows, and thrills with each other.

1. What has been the most exciting event in my friend's life lately?

2. What did I do to communicate my excitement for him?

3. Is there anything more that I could do?

Transparency #66

Supportive Precept 3:

Intimate friends must be willing to take on the responsibility of his becoming more like Christ.

1. What areas of my spiritual life could I improve in order to be a better example to my friend?

2. In what areas of his/her spiritual life can I play a better role of developing?

3. How can I begin this week?

Supportive Precept 4:

Intimate friends must be willing to die for one another.

Teacher's Note:

Go over the material on page 167 of the Discussion Manual.

Personal Application:

Encourage them to take home the papers on which they wrote the three names. Encourage them to pray for those three people every day this week. Remind them of some of the specific responsibilities they need to follow through on.

Closing Prayer:

Close by giving each a minute to pray silently for his potential friend, casual friend, and close friend. You close the meeting with prayer.

MAKING FRIENDS
Lesson 23

(Discussion Manual pages 168-75)

Introduction:

Have the students relate how their attempts at making a new friend went this week. You may have to pry this information out of them. If they did not follow through with their "Game Plan," reassign it to them.

As quickly as friendships can be made among teenagers, they can be destroyed. The tearing apart of a freindship will also include the tearing apart of hearts. God did not mean for us to hurt one another. Every time we do, we damage our walk with God. This lesson deals with the subject of broken friendships from two angles: (1) why it is so difficult to mend broken friendships and (2) steps that can be taken to mend broken friendships.

IV. Barriers to Overcome to Make Peace With Friends Who Have Hurt Us

Key Principles:

1. An exchange of cutting remarks makes mending a broken friendship difficult.

2. Getting revenge makes mending a broken friendship difficult.

3. An inability to swallow pride can make mending a broken friendship difficult.

4. We should be honest with God about the hard feelings we have toward our friends.

5. Search the Scripture for verses that teach you how to treat friends.

6. Confess your sins against your friend to the Lord.

7. Look at the misunderstanding from your friend's point of view.

8. Go to your friend and seek forgiveness.

Teacher's Note:

To begin this section, have each student think for a minute of a friend that he has either offended or was offended by. Tell the class it is important to mend those broken relationships. Even though a student may feel that his particular case is beyond repair, challenge them to open their hearts to God's mending Holy Spirit. Pray, asking God to mend many friendships as a result of this lesson.

Principle 1   (DM page 168):

An exchange of cutting remarks makes mending a broken friendship difficult.

Transparency #67

Teacher's Note:

Teach directly from pages 168-69 of the Discussion Manual.

Key Verse:

Proverbs 18:19

1. Why does this verse say it's easier to capture a fortified city than to win back a friend? (Answer: His anger is so strong that it won't let you deal with him rationally.)

2. What has to be done before you can defuse his anger? (Answer: You have to defuse your own anger.)

1 Peter 3:8-9

Principle 2   (DM page 169):

Getting revenge makes mending a broken friendship difficult.

Key Verse:

Romans 12:10

1. What are we trying to accomplish when we give someone the silent treatment? (Answer: We are saying that we don't need that person as part of our daily lives.)

2. Who else is affected by the silent treatment? (Answer: All of your mutual friends.)

3. Do you think the silent treatment is an immature response to a problem?

4. Why or why not?

Key Verse:

Proverbs 17:9

Project:

Play a round of the gossip game. (This usually works with five or more people.) Whisper some information in the first person's ear and have him pass it on. Have the last person say what he heard and compare it to what was really said. Follow with these questions:

1. Why is it that the farther a piece of information gets from a person, the more distorted it gets? (Answer: Because you are depending on people to: (1) hear it accurately and (2) transmit it accurately.)

2. What other factor comes into play when you tell another person how you were hurt by a friend? (Answer: Your personal prejudice enters the picture.)

Principle 3   (DM page 170);

An inability to swallow our pride can make mending a broken relationship difficult.

Key Verses:

Matthew 18:21-22

Do we ever have an excuse not to forgive a person who has hurt us?

Colossians 3:13

Teacher's Note:

Have the students answer the questions at the bottom of page 171 in their manuals. Give them about thirty seconds to ponder the last questions. Then have a time of silent prayer, urging them to use that time to ask God to take away the bitterness that is keeping them from forgiving their friends. Close the time with a simple "Amen."

Key Verses: (DM page 172):

Matthew 5:23-25

1. Why does God say to reconcile with your friend before you come to worship Him? (Answer: God wants you to worship Him with a pure heart.)

2. If it was the other guy's fault, why does God put the burden of responsibility on you to reconcile? (Answer: Because God is not as concerned about whose fault it is as He is about what is going to be done to bring peace back into the relationship.)

3. Why does He give the advice of verse 25? (Answer: You may be the one at fault. If you reconcile quickly, you may preclude more hostility.)

Teacher's Note:

Up to this point you have been discussing <u>why</u> it is hard to mend broken friendships. The last section of this lesson is devoted to <u>what</u> one should do to repair broken friendships. Have them think of a specific friendship that has been on the rocks. It may be the same one they had in mind at the beginning of this lesson. Encourage them to be honest in their hearts. Have each keep that person in mind as you go through the five steps to reconciliation.

V. How to Mend a Broken Friendship

Principle 4   (DM page 173):

We should be honest with God about the hard feelings we have toward our friend.

Key Verses:

Psalm 139:23-24

Teacher's Note:

This is not a time we go to God in an attempt to justify our actions. God knows who's right and who's wrong. This is a time for us to honestly admit that we are hurt, angry, or bitter. Anger and bitterness are sins, even if we were not guilty of the original offense.

Principle 5   (DM page 173):

Search the Scriptures for verses that teach you how to treat friends.

Teacher's Note:

There are ample verses on friendship in this chapter of the Discussion Manual. Suggest that your students spend some time on their own going back through this chapter, making a list of the Key Verses.

Principle 6   (DM page 174):

Confess your sin against your brother to the Lord.

Key Verse:

Psalm 51:4

1. What specific sins did I commit in this situation?

2. How have they hurt God?

3. Do I want those sins marring my fellowship?

4. Are the sins worth losing a good friend over?

Teacher's Note:

This line of questioning can help the student think through his specific problem. At this point in the lesson, it would be ideal to have them take care of this matter with the Lord. You decide what's best based on your situation. At the end of the lesson you will be encouraging them to follow through with these steps this week.

Principle 7   (DM page 174):

Look at the misunderstanding from your friend's point of view.

1. What caused this problem in the first place?

2. Is this misunderstanding worth losing a good friend over?

3. What needs has my friend been having that I've been unable to meet because of our disagreement?

Principle 8   (DM page 175):

Go to your friend and seek forgiveness.

Teacher's Note:

Explain the material under this principle. Reivew the five steps to mending a broken friendship.

Personal Application:

Pass out pieces of paper to everyone in the class. Instruct them to each write out a formal apology to the friend he has had a disagreement with. It should be brief, honest, and sincere. Remind them that this is not the time to determine blame or guilt. A suggested apology could go like this:

_____, please forgive me for sinning against you in our disagreement over _____. I don't want to be alienated from you over this. I consider your friendship a prized possession and desire to restore the excitement to our relationship once again. Therefore I extend to you this apology, and I will be grateful to be friends again._

Pray that God will give them the courage to either speak these words to their friends this week (ideally--today, Ephesians 4:26), or send this note to them today. If they send the note, they should follow it immediately with a face-to-face encounter.

Have them review the chapter on making friends this week. Remind them to list verses from it to refer to when they are experiencing hassles with friends. Again, emphasize their apology notes and challenge them to follow through with reconciliation. Close in prayer.

Closing Prayer:

If you know of any particular broken friendships with or among your students, you might want to make some phone calls this week to encourage them to follow through with the mending process.

HONESTY
Lesson 24

(Discussion Manual pages 177-89)

Introduction:

Teacher, this chapter could mark a turning point in the lives of some of your students. Counselors' offices are filled with Christians of all ages who have a basic problem with honesty. Among teenagers the problem is of epidemic proportions. Cheating in school is so commonplace that even Christian kids openly participate or fail to take a stand against it. The integrity of a man's word has also taken a beating in recent years. Because large segments of the adult community have allowed their credibility to be lowered by a lack of honesty, whole segments of the teenage population have adopted their parents' poor example as a way of life. As you prepare these lessons, pray that God will instill His character into you and your students, so that you will be known for your honesty.

Key Principles:

1. God is against lying because it goes against His pure nature of truth and faithfulness.

2. God is against lying because it was originated by and continues to take place because of Satan.

3. God is against lying because to tell a lie is to do the unloving thing.

4. God is against lying because it hurts the person who is lying.

Project A:

Using the three situations on pages 177 and 178 in the Discussion Manual, assume the role of the "devil's advocate." Take the wrong point of view on each situation and stand for it. That will accomplish a couple of goals.

1. It will give you an idea of what your students feel about dishonest behavior.

2. It will show you weak areas that need to be dealt with more thoroughly.

3. It will force the students to grapple with the delicate problems that accompany being honest (like getting your friends in trouble).

I.   The Basis for Honesty

Teacher's Note:

Review the definition of honesty at the top of page 179 in the manual. Begin outlining the chapter on an overhead transparency or poster board. The outline should contain all major headings and key Scriptures. It will serve as immediate reinforcement to what you have covered in the Discussion Manual, and will also be used later as a review tool. (Therefore, do it neatly and bring it back each week.)

Key Verses:

Deuteronomy 10:17-20

1. According to these verses, who determines what is right and wrong? (Answer: God.)

2. Are God's standards of right and wrong absolute (unchangeable)? (Answer: Yes.)

3. How do His absolute standards differ from the relative standards of modern thought? (Answer: <u>Relative</u> implies a changing or subjective standard that is determined by the individual. God has not told us to make up our own rules; He has told us the rules and expects us to obey them.)

Transition:

Because modern thinking has been rejecting God's absolute standards, man has become more and more prone to dishonesty. But God's standards remain the same. God wants us to be aware that He does not want us to be involved in any part of a lie.

Teacher's Note:

Have the students answer the questions on page 180 in their Discussion Manuals first, then have them share their answers out loud.

II. God Wants You to Know That He Does Not Wish for You to Be Involved in Any Part of a Lie

Principle 1   (DM page 181):

God is against lying because it goes against His pure nature of truth and faithfulness.

Transparency #68

Teacher's Note:

Remember to be writing the outline as you go along. (You could have it written out in advance, but covered up. Then simply expose the outline as you go along.) Cover the verses on page 181 in the manual, and then go over the definition of truth at the top of page 182. Have volunteers put this definition into their own words.

Key Verses:

1 Peter 2:22-23

1. Could Jesus have told a few "white lies" that would have kept Him from going through the crucifixion? (Answer: Sure, but Jesus' nature is to be absolutely truthful.)

2. Does that mean, then, that our total honesty could actually bring on problems for us? (Answer: Yes! In fact, it should be expected when you are dealing with a dishonest world.)

Transition:

Dishonesty runs counter to the very nature of God. If God is not the source of dishonesty, then who is? Our next principle points out from whom we inherited this problem.

Principle 2   (DM page 183):

God is against lying because it was originated by and continues to take place because of Satan.

Key Verse:

John 8:44

Teacher's Note:

Have the students answer the questions on page 183 in the Discussion Manual. Have the students give examples of things that Satan might say are all right, but which are really examples of his lying. (A few examples might be: sex is a beautiful thing and is OK between any consenting couple; parents are just as corrupt as we are, therefore we are not obligated to obey them; and the Bible is a good collection of myths and tales from which we can gain insights.)

If time permits, spend some time looking at man's fall into sin in the Garden of Eden. Help them see how Satan puts mild twists into God's Word to misrepresent Him.

Transition:

Lying is against God's holy nature. However, it is in complete harmony with Satan's nature. What's worse is that lying is an action that must involve other people. Because of that, lying does a lot of damage to people. Therefore . . .

Principle 3   *(DM page 184):*

   God is against lying because to tell a lie is to do the unloving thing.

Key Verse:

   Proverbs 25:18

Teacher's Note:

   Look through your newspaper and news magazines this week for articles that deal with people's not telling the truth. (There are usually plenty of examples each week.) Show them to the class at this time and discuss how those lies are damaging the people involved.

   Discuss the three types of people who are injured by a lie, and include that on the outline you are developing.

Project B:

   Debate the old saying, "Sticks and stones may break my bones, but words will never hurt me."

      1. Do you agree or disagree?

      2. How does this statement compare with Proverbs 25:18?

Supplemental Verses:

   James 3:3-10

      1. According to these verses, what is the hardest part of our body to control? (Answer: The tongue.)

      2. Why is it that the tongue is so difficult to control? (Answer: Verse 8--it is a restless evil and full of deadly poison.)

Transition:

   Lies are Satan's tools. When we lie, we involve ourselves in unloving action. Many people are injured by lies, but our last principle points out the one who suffers the most.

Principle 4   *(DM page 186):*

   God is against lying because it hurts the person who is lying.

Teacher's Note:

In the outline you are developing, include the three consequences for the person who lies. For the remainder of the lesson, teach directly through the material on pages 186-89 of the Discussion Manual. Use the following material as a supplement to the teaching on these pages.

Transparencys #69 — #70 — #71

Key Verses:

Galatians 6:7-8

1. When you sow a grain of wheat, what is unique about the product that it produces? (Answer: It produces wheat. But it is a stalk of wheat with a head that contains many more grains like the one planted.)

2. How is this an analogy of lying? (Answer: One lie fosters many more lies.)

3. What problems occur when our lies are multiplied? (Answer: We can't remember which lies we told to which people. We also have a hard time remembering the truth.)

Personal Application:

Memorize Proverbs 12:22 (DM page 189) together. After students have repeated it as a group two or three times, pair them up. Have them repeat the verse to each other. Have them pray in pairs for the following:

1. That they would be more committed to being honest.

2. That they would be more aware of the consequences of dishonesty.

3. That they would be committed to absolute honesty among their peer group this week.

Closing Prayer:

Close in prayer when they are done.

HONESTY
Lesson 25

(Discussion Manual pages 190-99)

Introduction:

The beginning of this lesson deals with practical steps that we should follow to keep us from lying. Since this goes with the material from the last lesson, a brief review is in order. Using the chart that you developed last time, highlight the <u>main points</u> of the outline. Use your own words to briefly explain what each point means. Tell them that the first thing you want to look at in this lesson is what to do when you are tempted to lie.

Key Principles:

1. When you are tempted to lie, remember that God cannot lie, hates lies, and will not condone falsehood in any form.

2. When you are tempted to lie, remember that to lie is to be at that moment a partner with the devil.

3. When you are tempted to lie, think of the damage you will do to others.

4. When you are tempted to lie, think of the good consequences of telling the truth.

5. God is against stealing because it shows unbelief in His character.

6. God is against stealing because we hurt ourselves when we steal.

7. God is against stealing because we use others when we steal.

Teacher's Note:

Have the students, without looking at their discussion manuals, suggest principles that they should think of when they are tempted to lie. List them on an overhead or chalkboard. Use this as a test to see how well they are grasping the material and as an indicator of the areas you need to emphasize as you teach through pages 190-93.

Principle 1   *(DM page 190);*

When you are tempted to lie, remember that God cannot lie, hates lies, and will not condone falsehood in any form.

Transparency #72

Teacher's Note:

Continue to complete an outline of this chapter on an overhead or poster board. This will be used for review purposes.

Supplemental Verses:

John 14:6

1 Peter 2:22-23

1 John 5:7

1. If I choose to lie, how will that make God feel?

2. If I choose to lie, what will it say about my relationship to God?

3. If I choose to lie, what impression of a Christian will I leave with people?

4. If I choose to lie, how will it affect my fellowhsip with God?

Key Verses:

1 Peter 1:14-16

Principle 2 *(DM page 191):*

When you are tempted to lie, remember that to lie is to be at that moment a partner with the devil.

Transparency #73

Supplemental Verse:

John 8:44

1. If I choose to lie, how will it make Satan feel?

2. If I choose to lie, what will it say about my attitude toward Satan?

3. If I choose to lie, how does it affect Satan's strategy for nullifying God's work in the world?

Key Verse:

James 4:7

1. Do we have to resist Satan alone? (Answer: No.)

2. What provision has God made for us to overcome Satan? (Answer: The Holy Spirit--John 15:15-18.)

Principle 3   (DM page 191):

When you are tempted to tell a lie, think of the damage that you will do to others.

Supplemental Verse:

Proverbs 25:18

1. If I choose to lie, how will it affect by credibility?

2. If I choose to lie, what will it do to the person to whom I'm lying?

3. If I choose to lie, what will it do to the person that I'm lying about?

Key Verses:

Psalm 34:11-14

Teacher's Note:

Take a minute to have your students relate some incidents in their lives in which lies have hurt people.

Principle 4   (DM page 192):

When you are tempted to lie, think of the good consequences of telling the truth.

Teacher's Note:

Clarify to your students that the best "lie detector" available is the truth. The truth will always coincide with the facts. The truth will always intimidate liars.

Teach through the four benefits of telling the truth on pages 192-93 in the manual. Highlight the verses that go with them.

Project:

Pass out different colored pieces of construction paper, colored pens, and scissors. Have the students make a "Lying Stifling Chart." Included on the chart should be the four steps to take when you're tempted to lie, a Scripture reference *for each, and the four benefits of step 4. Have the students make them attractive to look at. When they have been completed, encourage the students to put them where they can be a constant reminder (on their mirrors, inside their locker doors, etc.)*

Transition:

Another form of dishonesty is stealing. Stealing is done many ways, but each time it disappoints God. For the remainder of this lesson we want to look at this problem.

Transparency #74

Teacher's Note:

Have students tell about the cheating problem at their schools. This will probably be a very "eye-opening" discussion and will give you plenty of reference material for this study. When you are done with this discussion, discuss the definition of stealing on page 193. Read down the list on the top of page 194. Have your students expand the list.

III. *God Wants You to Know That He is Completely Against Your Being Involved in Any Type of Stealing*

Principle 5   *(DM page 193):*

God is against stealing because it shows unbelief in His character.

Teacher's Note:

Point out that a person steals things that he thinks he needs. However, in most cases he is really stealing things that he <u>wants</u>. Discuss the difference between needs and wants, and the motivation behind each. Next discuss the <u>real</u> problem behind cheating in school. Is it that God is not willing to help us, or is it that we are too lazy to put forth the effort necessary to achieve academically?

Key Verse:

1 Corinthians 10:13

Teacher's Note:

Have your students answer the questions to this verse. Assign it as a verse to be memorized this week. Tell them you will check to see how well they are doing on it next lesson.

Transition:

Stealing, like lying, offends the very character of God. It also is dangerous to the person who steals and the person who is stolen from. That is brought out in our next two principles.

Principle 6   *(DM page 197):*

God is against stealing because we hurt ourselves when we steal.

Transparency #75

Key Verse:

Proverbs 20:17

Illustration: Dr. Madison Saratt, a mathematics professor at Vanderbilt University, used to admonish his class before a test by saying something like this: "Today I am giving two examinations, one in trigonometry, and the other in honesty. I hope you will pass them both. If you must fail one, fail trigonometry. There are many good people in the world who can't pass trig, but there are no good people in the world who cannot pass the examination of honesty."

Key Verse:

Proverbs 16:8

   1.   What are some of the benefits of taking a lower grade on a test, but
        earning the grade honestly?

   2.   What are some of the liabilities of getting good grades dishonestly?

   3.   If you were having open heart surgery, which would you rather have:
        a doctor who made excellent grades in medical school but cheated to
        get them, or a doctor who made average grades but earned his grades
        honestly? Why?

Principle 7   *(DM page 199);*

God is against stealing because we use others when we steal.

Key Verses:

Philippians 2:3-4

1. *How does cheating affect test scores that are graded on a "curve"? (Answer: The honest students could end up with average or below average grades because cheaters threw the curve off and claimed the top grades.)*

2. *How does stealing affect the clothes, food, and merchandise that we buy? (Answer: Billions of dollars worth of stolen good are paid for by honest consumers every year.)*

3. *How does stealing affect our taxes and our personal safety? (Answer: More of our tax dollars have to go to pay for more police to combat theft. Burglaries are happening more and more each year, many resulting in injury and death to innocent people.)*

Personal Application / Closing Prayer:

Have the students bow their heads and think about the three principle on stealing as you read them back to them. Next have them think of any ways that they have stolen or cheated lately. Invite them to pray along with you in their hearts the following prayer of repentance:

> *Dear Father, forgive me for the times that I've stolen lately. I know that stealing hurts you, it hurts me, and it hurts a lot of innocent people. I want to be honest in all of my endeavors. So help me through your Holy Spirit. Thank you, in Jesus' name. Amen.*

HONESTY
Lesson 26

(Discussion Manual pages 199-202)

Introduction:

This lesson covers the last three and a half pages in the Discussion Manual. A review will precede the lesson. You have two options: (1) You can have a thorough review and culminate the lesson by covering this material, or (2) you can have a brief review, and a brief lesson, leaving time to use as you see fit.

Prepare a chart showing the Key Principles, Scriptures, and subpoints from this chapter on honesty. Review the chart, emphasizing the material on stealing.

Next, review the memory verse that they were assigned (1 Corinthians 10:13).

Key Principles:

1. Share your problem of stealing (or cheating) with a close Christian friend.

2. Think of the consequences of stealing.

3. Involve yourself in productive activities in the place of stealing.

4. Learn to be content with what you have.

Transition:

Any of us are capable of stealing. If we find ourselves being influenced to steal, there are specific things that we can do.

IV. What Can We Do If We Find Ourselves Caught in the Trap of Stealing (or Cheating)?

Principle 1   (DM page 199):

Share your problems of stealing (or cheating) with a close Christian friend.

Teacher's Note:

The person that they choose should be discreet, and capable of helping. Suggest some people in your church or fellowship that might be good for your students.

Principle 2   (DM page 200):

Think of the consequences of stealing.

Transparency #76

Teacher's Note:

Cut out newspaper and magazine clippings that tell of people's reaping the bitter results of dishonest gain. Cover the material on the rest of the page.

Principle 3   (DM page 201):

Involve yourself in productive activities in the place of stealing.

Transparency #77

Teacher's Note:

Have your students answer the questions. In answering the second question, have them think of creative alternatives to specific kinds of stealing. For instance:

1. Cheating in school--learning how to study, getting a **tutor**.

2. Stealing clothes--learning how to sew.

3. Stealing money--getting a part-time job.

Principle 4   (DM page 202):

Learn to be content with what you have.

Transparency #78

Supplemental Verses:

Philippians 4:11-13

Personal Application:

Give each student a piece of paper. Have the group complete a "Personal Contentment Inventory." Have them number to 20. Beside each number have them write the name of something that they have that is adequate for their needs (although not necessarily what they would like it to be). The list could include people, personal gifts, their geographic location. Give them five minutes to complete their inventory.

Closing Prayer:

Have the students read down their lists, thanking God for each item. Close in prayer.

> Dear Father, You have given me so much to be thankful for. Help me to keep my focus on the good things that I have-- not the unnecessary things that I want. Help me to realize that You have given me all that I ever need in giving me the gift of Your Son, in whose name I pray. Amen.

RELATIONSHIPS VOLUME 1

1. **Understanding the Bible, A Counseling Book**
God intends for man to be happy and fulfilled, but man has ignored God's Counsel. This chapter discusses this problem by showing how the value and wisdom of the Bible was meant to be experienced in everyday life.

2. **Knowing God's Will**
Who should I marry? What school should I attend? What vocation should I pursue? These are questions students are asking, so this chapter outlines ways students can seek and know God's will for their lives.

3. **Balanced Self-Image**
This chapter shares how God views us and gives practical steps in forming a healthy, balanced view of ourselves.

4. **Dealing with Loneliness**
One of the most widespread problems among American students is loneliness. What is loneliness? What steps can students take to get out of loneliness? This chapter will help.

5. **Understanding Parents**
Few relationships effect students' lives as do parental relationships. Common problems between teens and parents and the Biblical solutions are adequately covered in this chapter.

6. **Understanding Sex**
This chapter deals with the rationale of God's view of sex, and His instructions for sex.

7. **Understanding Dating**
A chapter giving insights into questions like: What are the problems that come up in dating? What qualities should I look for in a date? Does God have a plan for my date life?

8. **Understanding Love**
This chapter defines the differences between love and infatuation by using 1 Corinthians 13 as its outline.

9. **Clearing the Mind**
Thinking pure and godly thoughts is not easy, especially for today's teenagers. This chapter discusses how the mind is the battleground for Satan, how students can achieve victory and how to glorify God with the mind.

10. **Dealing with Temptation**
Being tempted and knowing who tempts us is not always easy to recognize. This chapter gives practical insights into the whole area of temptation.

Gives Instructors of Bible and Christian Ethics Classes:

- 26 Lessons Providing a Semester of Material
- Over 30 Projects for Individuals and Groups
- Additional Bible References
- Hundreds of Discussion Questions
- Many Illustrations and Applications
- Lesson Aims and Key Principles
- And, Teaching Tips Built-In

Available For:

- Student Relationships—Volume 1
- Student Relationships—Volume 2
- Student Relationships—Volume 3

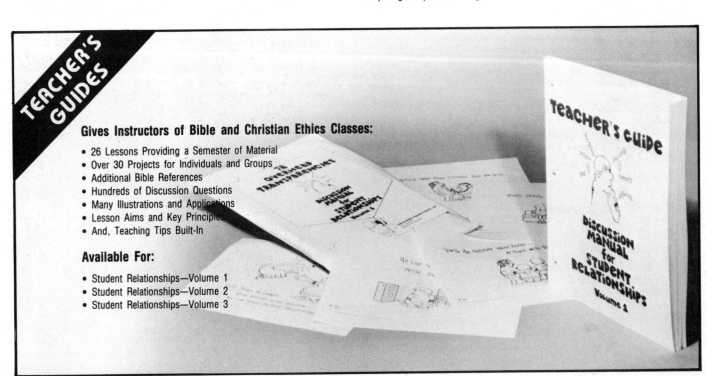

RELATIONSHIPS VOLUME 2

1. How to Glorify God
Glorifying God and how to do it can be difficult to understand and teach. This chapter gets to the heart of what glorifying God is all about.

2. Discipleship
This chapter shares the answers to the questions: What are the costs and characteristics of being a true disciple of Jesus? How can I become a disciple of Jesus Christ?

3. Love
Why love is so important and what is real love, are answered according to the description of love in 1 Corinthians 13.

4. What Love is Not
This chapter explains what seven things love is not, including jealousy, bragging, arrogance, seeking its own, etc.

5. Questions on Dating
The author of the manual, Dawson McAllister, answers questions high school students across the country ask on dating. This chapter actually takes many of those questions and answers them honestly and according to Scripture.

6. Peer Group Pressure
One of the strongest influences in students' lives are the thoughts and actions of peers towards them. In this discussion students will learn how to identify this pressure and deal with it.

7. Making Friends
This chapter teaches students how to make friends and what types of friends God desires for them to have.

8. Honesty
Honesty is often rejected in a world where personal gain is more important than trustworthiness. Here you will investigate the results of being dishonest and the benefits of honesty.

RELATIONSHIPS VOLUME 3

1. How to Deal with Cliques
This chapter deals with the ever common problem of cliques, what God has to say about cliques and how to deal with bitterness toward the elite.

2. What to do When Your Boyfriend or Girlfriend "Drops You"
Being rejected by someone we date and care about is very difficult to handle. This chapter relates how to deal with broken hearts.

3. God's View of the Misuse of Drugs and Alcohol
This in-depth discussion shares why God is absolutely against the misuse of drugs and alcohol. A positive answer to the problem is given—the person of Jesus Christ.

4. How to Break Bad Habits
Recognizing bad habits and learning how to break them is the topic of this chapter. Deep and practical truths are explained to the Christian on how to gain victory over sin.

5. How to Develop New Healthy Habits
This important section, in a very practical way, explains how the student can begin forming new and healthy habits. Two key projects are included to help students put the teaching into effect.

6. How to Live in a Broken Home
Living in a broken home and allowing God's love to mend some of the hurts is not easy. This chapter gives some valuable insights into this widespread problem and it lists how the student can deal with the situation realistically.

7. How to Deal with Guilt
Every student at one time or another faces the emotional pressure of guilt. This section simply shares how God views guilt and helps the student deal with it. It's a must for every youth worker who does counseling.

8. The Christian Student and Rock Music
The authors give insight into the advantages and disadvantages of listening to rock music and some creative alternatives.

9. Disciplining Your Time
This chapter deals with laziness, time wasting activities, how God wants us to spend our time, and practical steps on how to make the most of our time.

10. How to Face Death
One thing we will all experience is death. This chapter answers the questions: What is death? Why is there death? Where does one go when he/she dies? What has God done about dying?

Student manuals are consumable due to fill-in-the-blanks, question responses and projects.

DISCUSSION MANUAL for STUDENT DISCIPLESHIP

GOD

WRITTEN BY
DAWSON McALLISTER
AND
DAN WEBSTER

Volume 1

DISCIPLESHIP VOLUME 1

Discussion Manual for Student Discipleship

Written By Dawson McAllister and John Miller

Volume 2

DISCIPLESHIP VOLUME 2

1. **The Importance of Obedience**
   This chapter reveals our responsibilities to God in regards to living successful Christian lives in front of the world.
2. **Learning to Obey God**
   The theme of chapter 1 continues in this chapter, with specific applications concerning our obedience to the Lord.
3. **Worship**
   The meaning of worship as a lifestyle is defined, with ways to worship also being explored.
4. **The Christian and the Lordship of Christ**
   The very essence of the Christian life is the Lordship of Jesus Christ. The chapter centers on learning to let Christ be Lord of our lives and how His Lordship is the key.
5. **The Christian Life and Endurance**
   Many Christians begin their new lives in Christ in a blaze of glory but end up in disaster. This chapter deals with the Christian's endurance and eventual victory in the race of life.
6. **The Responsibilities of Love**
   Learning to love one another in Christ can be difficult, but it is essential. This chapter handles the attitudes of submission, servanthood and active loving.
7. **Our Responsibility Toward Other Christians**
   Developing love is the highest goal, so this chapter discusses the negative attitudes and actions to avoid.
8. **How to Start Your Own Ministry**
   This chapter gives helpful and creative ways of having a ministry. Covers qualifications of ministry, costs involved and how to begin a personal ministry.

Student manuals are consumable due to fill-in-the-blanks, question responses and projects.

Have you ever wondered how to explain to your students what the Cross of Jesus Christ was all about? It's the most important doctrine of our faith.

Follow Jesus' steps from the shocking moments of the Last Supper, when a betrayer is announced . . . through the ripping pain in Gethsemane . . . to the tragedy of the unfair trials . . .to the life and death encounter with Pilate . . .and finally, through the awesome, agonizing six hours on the Cross!

Take your students on the most important walk in history!

Each chapter highlights an event that led the Son of God one step closer to death.

1. Jesus Christ, More Than a Good Man
2. Sorrow and the Last Supper
3. On to the Agony in Gethsemane
4. Arrest and Compassion
5. Injustice and the Religious Trials
6. Desertion and Denial
7. On Trial and Bound at Daybreak
8. Questioned by Pilate and Herod
9. Condemned by Pilate, the Crowd-Fearing Coward
10. Man's Worst, God's Best at the Cross
11. Abuse and Love on the Cross
12. "It is Finished!"

Continue the journey from the Cross when the temple veil is torn in two and Christ's side is pierced . . . witness the loving preparation of Christ's body . . . discover the rolled away stone from the empty tomb . . . meet the risen Christ face to face . . . unravel the scandalous bribery of the Roman guards . . . observe the bodily appearances of Jesus . . . hear His last words and see the ascension. Plus, the final two chapters deal with the apologetical view of the Resurrection and what this historical reality means to believers today.

Help your students get a clear understanding of the cornerstone of the Christian faith—the Resurrection. A Walk with Christ Through the Resurrection is a discussion manual made simple. Students are projected into the events surrounding Christ prior to and after His Resurrection by thought-jarring questions and 80 realistic illustrations.

Students will be able to learn and discuss with each other why the Resurrection is significant and what it means to them.

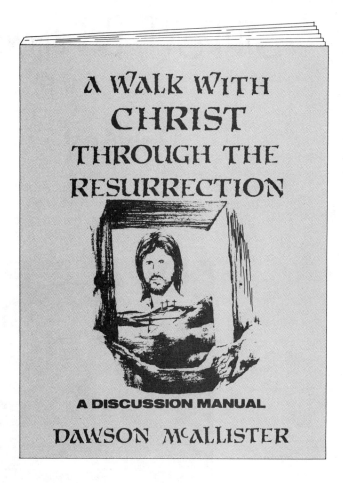

Continue the exhilarating journey from the Cross to the Ascension!

Each chapter highlights an event that led the Messiah through the Resurrection.

1. Why is the Resurrection Important?
2. Loving Preparation of the Body
3. The Empty Tomb
4. Face to Face with the Risen Christ
5. Bribery of the Guard
6. Christ Appears Before the Disciples
7. Jesus Comforts and Teaches
8. The Last Commands and Ascension
9. How Do We Know Christ Rose?
10. What Does the Resurrection Mean?

STuDeNT ReLaTioNShiPs CoNFeReNce
WiTH
DaWSoN   McALLisTeR

The goal of Shepherd Productions is to be a servant to the local
youth worker in his efforts to disciple and win students to Christ.
One of the key ministries of Shepherd Productions is the Student
Relationships Conference with Dawson McAllister.

Dawson, a nationally known youth speaker, lectures each night on
selected topics dealing with the problems facing the American
student and God's answers to those problems. Areas such as loneliness, self image, guilt, bad habits, broken homes, rock music,
drugs and alcohol, cliques, peer group pressure, infatuation and
others are discussed.

DAWSON McALLISTER YOUTH MANUALS

ORDER FORM

Date_____

SHIP TO:

Name_____ Position_____

PLEASE PRINT OR TYPE

Organization_____ Phone No._____

Address_____

City_____ State_____ Zip_____

SHIP: Unless specified otherwise, will ship Parcel Post.

BILL TO:

Name_____

Address_____ Phone No._____

City_____ State_____ Zip_____

P.O. No._____

For office use only: | | | | | | — | | | |

disciple-ship

God's answers to students' needs

topical studies

relation-ships and issues

RELATIONSHIPS MANUALS

	Student			Teacher			78 Transparencies		
	Code	Price	Qty	Code	Price	Qty	Code	Price	Qty
Discussion Manual for Student Relationships, Vol. 1	2010	7.95		2011	5.95		2080	39.95	
Discussion Manual for Student Relationships, Vol. 2	2012	7.95		2013	5.95		2081	39.95	
Discussion Manual for Student Relationships, Vol. 3	2014	7.95		2015	5.95		2082	39.95	

DISCIPLESHIP MANUALS

	Student					
	Code	Price	Qty			
Discussion Manual for Student Discipleship, Vol. 1	2020	7.95				
Discussion Manual for Student Discipleship, Vol. 2	2022	7.95				

TOPICAL STUDIES

	Student			Teacher			36 Transparencies		
	Code	Price	Qty	Code	Price	Qty	Code	Price	Qty
A Walk With Christ to the Cross: A Discussion Manual	2030	7.95		2031	5.95		2085	22.95	
A Walk With Christ Through the Resurrection: A Discussion Manual	2032	7.95							

ORDERING INFORMATION: Please allow 3 weeks for delivery.

Postage & Handling: Add 7% of total amount
Minimum charge: $1.50
Special Handling or Air Shipments extra

Returns: All sales are final except:
a. Defective materials may be returned for full credit.
b. Up to 15% of total order may be returned for full credit, if returned in saleable condition within 60 days from date of invoice.

Terms: Cash with order or 30 days net for charge sales.

Prices: **Prices are subject to change without notice.**

ORDERING SUMMARY

Sub Total	
Postage & Handling	
Total Amount	

☐ Payment enclosed
☐ Please bill

ROPER PRESS, INC.

915 Dragon   Dallas, Texas 75207 (214) 742-6696